The True Eightfold Path

IRH PRESS

The True
Eightfold
Guideposts Path
for
Self-Innovation

Ryuho Okawa

IRH Press

BOOKS
IRH PRESS
New York

ISBN 13: 978-1-942125-80-8
ISBN 10: 1-942125-80-1

Printed in Canada

First Edition

Contents

Chapter 1

Introduction

The Meaning and Prerequisite of Self-Reflection

Chapter 2

Right View

Chapter 3
Right Thought

Chapter 4
Right Speech

Chapter 5

Right Action

Chapter 6
Right Living

Chapter 7
Right Effort

Chapter 8
Right Will

Chapter 9
Right Meditation

Chapter 10
General Statement
The Significance of the Eightfold Path in Today's World

What Is the Purpose of the True Eightfold Path?

PREFACE TO THE
NEW AND REVISED EDITION

The original issue of this book was based on a series of four consecutive lectures the author gave thirty-one years ago at the age of thirty-two at Happy Science Training Hall in Nishiogi, Tokyo.

The contents of this book are of a contemporary nature so that novices will be able to easily understand them.

The Four Noble Truths – Birth, Aging, Illness, and Death – and the Eightfold Path can be considered the main pillars of Buddhism, the teachings of Shakyamuni Buddha. These two concepts are combined and simply called "the Four Noble Truths and the Eightfold Path." In following this path, it has been considered that the state of "the Middle Way" is achieved, and Wisdom is obtained.

This book makes use of the clarity of the original edition, incorporates updates on Happy Science's development over the past thirty-one years, and gives explanatory comments from the perspective of fundamental Buddhist thoughts. I am very pleased to publish this new edition in a more engaging style.

Ryuho Okawa
Master & CEO of Happy Science Group
May 30, 2020

PREFACE

I am very pleased to have the opportunity to put together this book, *The True Eightfold Path*, as a theoretical pillar for the discipline of self-reflection at Happy Science.

This book is based on a series of four consecutive lectures on self-reflection training I gave to learners of intermediate and advanced levels at Happy Science Training Hall in January this year. I think I have managed to explain thoroughly what self-reflection is from a modern perspective.

I sincerely wish that my readers will be able to take guidance from this book to achieve self-innovation, build a new way of living, and revitalize their lives.

Ryuho Okawa
Master & CEO of Happy Science Group
March 1989

Chapter 1

Introduction

The Meaning and Prerequisite of Self-Reflection

Lecture given on January 7, 1989
at Happy Science Training Hall, Tokyo

1

What Is Self-Reflection?

Why is self-reflection required?

In this book, titled *The True Eightfold Path*, I would like to discuss my own contemporary interpretation of the "Eightfold Path" and how methods of self-reflection should be considered.

Why is self-reflection necessary now? Have you ever thought about this in depth? Has anything ever caused you to think about it? When you ask yourself such questions, you might very likely regret having lived so many years of life without thinking deeply. As ordinary human beings, many of you would probably think like that.

I would like to first consider why there can be a concept such as self-reflection, and why it is necessary.

You have already learned from various teachings of the Truth, spiritual messages, and interviews that you live in an eternal cycle of reincarnation. You must have heard that since a long time ago, you have been experiencing reincarnations in cycles of hundreds or even thousands of years.

The question I would like to raise first is, "If you have read of such things in my books, have you taken them to be merely pieces of knowledge to skim through or have you taken them as wisdom that you can understand in the depth of your soul, truths that you can clearly recognize and are in total agreement with?"

The importance of asking yourself daily, "Who am I?"

If reincarnation is not just theory or an analogy, but true fact, what kind of life should you live while on Earth? How should you live?

I would say that you should look at what is happening now from a point at infinity.

There are two perspectives concerning this "point at infinity."

The first is a view from the past. It is the perspective of looking at the present from the time you first began life as a human being. The other is the perspective of looking at the present from the future hundreds or thousands of years from now, after the coming decades when all of you, without exception, will have left this world on Earth.

From these two viewpoints in time, from the past and the future, we must look at how we are doing in the present.

It is necessary to understand that this is the actual foundation of self-reflection. Self-reflection is more than just a practice. It is not just theoretical thinking, nor is it something that is considered from a moral perspective.

Self-reflection is associated with the fact that you were given eternal life by God. The fact that you live an eternal life provides you with a perspective of looking at the present from the distant past and from far into the future.

So what does self-reflection mean in the end? It means knowing who you are. You should wake up and be aware of this. I am saying that you must not forget to daily ask yourself the question, "Who am I?"

2

What Does It Mean to Be a Human Being?

In the distant past, part of God's consciousness was dispersed widely, and with the ideal of creating human beings, this widespread consciousness became individualized in human form. Each person has such an origin, and a history of having been born into a physical body and having gone through spiritual training on various planets. Some of you may think you have only experienced life on planet Earth. However, in the continuous and essential flow of souls, you would also have experienced soul training on other planets in the distant past.

Why is there the possibility of reincarnation beyond the boundaries of a single planet, let alone reincarnation centering on Earth? Through such experiences, what is God trying to offer you? We must think about this.

There are the secrets of the creation of the universe and of humans. Without the perspective of thinking deeply about both of these secrets, you would no longer be allowed to be human.

Therefore, I would like you to first ponder whether you accept the fact that you are a human being. What does it mean to learn and accept that you are born human, actually living, thinking, and being allowed to live?

It means that you must first know that you are a "created existence." You need to know that you are both created and purposeful.

You are not just simply created like a chair or a desk made for a specific purpose. You are a created being, and this being is living an eternal life with a great purpose. You need to know that you belong in such a spiritual flow.

When you think of this fact, you can have a different perspective.

3

What Is the Starting Point of Self-Reflection?

Exploration of the Right Mind begins with faith

I believe you are studying the four criteria that comprise the Principles of Happiness of love, wisdom, self-reflection, and progress. It can be understood that the "self-reflection" refers to a component of the Principles of Happiness.

However, it is necessary to consider that there is a deeper aspect to it and that a more solid foundation might be essential.

This is what I would like to emphasize: The four ideas of love, wisdom, self-reflection, and progress are not to be explored independently and separately. Nor are they considered unrelated to each other as if they were floating like distinct icebergs scattered over the ocean.

So what is the foundation on which the Principles of Happiness are built? There should be something that lies underneath. In truth, what lies at the base of these principles is faith.

"Faith" may present a strong image of worshiping a divine being that exists somewhere far beyond, or of asking for help from some other power.

However, what is the origin of faith? It lies in the secret of creation, that you were created by God. Do you believe that you were created by God? Do you believe that you are undergoing spiritual training with eternal life through repeated cycles of reincarnation? You are confronted with such questions.

When you believe this, it is the beginning of faith. Nothing starts without faith. Based on the foundation of faith, the paths of love, wisdom, self-reflection, and progress exist. So does Exploration of the Right Mind. All of these ideas have faith as their foundation.

Therefore, you should not consider faith as something simplistic. Nor should you consider it merely a commonplace notion. Instead, faith is something deeper and more fundamental.

This "faith" I am talking about is not what is described conventionally. I would say that faith means recognizing what is fact and confirming the truth. It would show that you have seen a portion of great wisdom and that you have understood how it works.

If you say that you have seen great wisdom, then you will accept it, agree with it, and believe in it. These are acts of faith.

Faith is completely different from praying for something magical. It is to know the secrets of the creation of the universe and humankind, and to understand them as authentic. This is the premise of faith.

Those who do not accept this premise will not be able to gain anything even if they read books about the Truth, or listen to my lectures on the Truth. I would say, "Be sure to build a foundation first."

First, recognize that
you are living in a world created by God

In the first days of Happy Science, I did not talk much about faith. This was because the word "faith" was viewed with bias. At Happy Science, it was certainly necessary to teach faith in our own way, but I was very wary that it would be seen in exactly the same manner as traditional religions.

However, Truth essentially has a very sturdy framework; there is no room for anyone to question this, nor is there any possibility for its foundation to be shaken. It is also something that cannot be criticized or analyzed. The facts that humans are created by God and live with eternal goals are truths that allow no debate.

Because they are facts and will not allow for any debate, there is no other way but to believe. Believing is about "taking a leap and accepting" and "seizing hold of" truths. Nothing else is allowed.

By taking this first step, a contract is created. In Western terms, this is bonding with God and a testament of belief. This is the start of learning.

At Happy Science, I talk about the three-step methodology in search of the Truth: exploration, study, and missionary work. By this, I do not mean undertaking an exploration like a natural scientist or doing research that involves looking at bacteria under a microscope. Nor do I teach people to believe in things that are only convenient for them and to reject what is not.

Essentially, it all starts from recognizing the solid foundation of living in a world created by God. Then to follow various explorations in the study of the Truth within the world of God. You must understand that those who do not satisfy this fundamental condition would not be allowed to enter the world of exploration for the Truth, nor would they be allowed to study. The precondition for you to study the Truth is to believe in God.

The mindset that is expected of those who enter the path of Truth

I have no intention of treating faith lightly. I do not want those without faith, in the sense that I have just discussed, to claim that they are studying the Truth in Happy Science and practicing spiritual discipline. It would be a big mistake to think it acceptable to regard Truth as merely printed information and skim through it. However, if you recognize yourself as one exploring the Truth, then I would like you to make a conviction to pursue it on a path based on a solid foundation.

It should be understood that those who are about to step forward as explorers will be placed in a very difficult position; this position is an uncompromising standpoint. You are about to know what God truly is. You are also about to know the real shape of yourselves as children of God, the children of Buddha. It is the same as standing on the ridge dividing life and death.

It is not my intent to mirror Zen Buddhism in any way, but I would like to say that unless you have such a conviction, you cannot understand the Truth, nor can you enter the path of enlightenment.

Do not enter the path of Truth without firm intention. If you attempt to take this path in a casual manner, it might be better to turn back now. If you are interested in becoming a disciple with the conviction to study the Truth seriously, then you should be well prepared for it.

I would like you to begin your study by having a true faith in God or Buddha as the starting point. If you cannot pass this stage, it would still be good to study the Truth more generally, as information, or just read my books. This may be another option you wish to take at this time.

I want to make this point clear.

4

The Prerequisite of Self-Reflection – The Spirit of Devotion to the Three Treasures

Shakyamuni Buddha taught this about 2,600 years ago. Among the readers of this book, a large number must have heard what he said at the time, which was, "To become my disciple, you must pledge your devotion to the Three Treasures."

This means to pledge devotion to Buddha, to the Dharma, which are the laws Buddha taught, and to the Sangha, abiding by the rules of Buddhist monastic order. Those who could not follow these three points were not admitted as trainees, and this is still the case.

If one entered this path as a trainee but had no intention to abide in the spirit of devotion to the Three Treasures, then that person was sent into the mountains for a week to undergo thorough self-reflection. And if that person was not able to repent, the person was then asked to leave the Order and return to being a lay believer. In Shakyamuni Buddha's Order, those who were unable to keep up with the required discipline were recommended to leave the Order and return to secular life.

With the comment that people who do not understand this premise would not be allowed to start self-reflection, nor would they be qualified to do so, I would like to end this introductory chapter.

Chapter 2

Right View

正
見

Lecture given on January 7, 1989
at Happy Science Training Hall, Tokyo

1

Responsibilities Associated with Seeing

Reformation of our mindsets in terms of "seeing" is needed

The first path in the Eightfold Path is Right View, which is to say, "seeing rightly." The practice of seeing rightly can be very difficult. This is because you are usually unaware that "seeing" is active work or a purposeful activity.

You usually think of seeing in the following way: When you wake up in the morning and open your eyes, you receive images on the retinas of your eyes. You spend the day mindlessly tracking the images that appear on the retinas. At the end of the day, you totally forget what has been pictured on them.

Therefore, it is necessary to first change that kind of mindset.

You are asked, "Although you have been given sight by God, through His arrangement involving your parents, have you ever determined what the functions of the eyes are for? What is the purpose of your eyes?"

Are they just to avoid falling down on the street? Are they used just to walk safely on the street? Are they only for opening your front door? Do you really think that your eyes are just for such insignificant matters? These questions serve as challenges.

They would lead you to the realization of how careless you have been concerning the role of your eyes. Your eyes have been used to see, but have not fully fulfilled their true potential.

Discovering God's intentions through visual images

What you see through your eyes is the world that God created. How do you measure the world He created? How do you judge it? How do you see it? This is an issue that only you are responsible for.

The world is what has been created. However, it is entirely up to each person to determine how the world and the people who live in it are viewed. And no one will question your responsibility based on how you appraise the scenes you see.

No one will complain about the way you judge the images you see. It is entirely up to each individual. It seems that you are not held responsible for the way you feel about a flower, whether you think it is beautiful or not, or for the way you feel about the scenery outside.

However, in truth, this world does not allow you to be so irresponsible.

As long as you have eyes that are functioning, there is a purpose. So what is the purpose? It is to discover God's intentions through visual images.

The reason that sight is so important is that of all sensory organs, the eyes serve as the best way to recognize the world.

Of course, there is the sense of smell that you can perceive through your nose. With the sense of smell, you may be able to tell the difference between animals, plants, or people. But the world that is discerned with the sense of smell is very narrow and can be ambiguous. For this purpose, the sense of smell is much less effective compared to vision.

There is also the sense of taste, but what can be detected by taste is extremely limited.

Then there is the sense of hearing, which is relatively important. "Hearing" is not clearly stated as a practice in the Eightfold Path, but if you attempt to categorize it, it would come under Right Thought, which I will discuss later. How can information obtained through hearing be analyzed? The answer is that you can construct your thoughts based on information you have heard, so hearing can be considered part of Right Thought.

2

Seeing the Work of God

The eyes contribute greatly to spiritual evolution and awakening

Notably, Right View being placed first in the Eightfold Path is linked to the most important of human sense organs, the eyes; they make the greatest contribution in perceiving the world.

Compared to the eyes, the sense of touch, for example, is not adequate to recognize the world fully. I am sure you will realize how much your sight contributes to your spiritual growth and awakening.

If you are to choose only one sense organ to help you understand, then please think about how much your eyes help you to recognize that you are living as a human being.

Even if you do not speak or hear so much as the result of physical impairment, you can still see what is going on in the world. But those who are born blind would experience extreme difficulties in understanding this world. It would be difficult to recognize what human beings are. It would also be difficult to recognize animals or plants. Being unable to see would be associated with such difficulties.

The "view" in Right View means to "look at" rather than just "see"

Right View in the true sense means to increase your level of understanding of what you see. You are expected to notice what is behind things, instead of seeing and accepting them as only images. In other words, you are expected to witness the work of God. You are expected to "look at the work of the hand of God, to look at the results of His work."

Those who cannot gain insight like this would fall short of claiming that they have lived as a child of God or a child of Buddha and observed the world. It would be merely that their eyes were open; they could not claim that they observed the world.

It may be related to the difference between "seeing" and "looking at" in English. Right View implies "looking at," or observation. It is not just using your visual ability to "see," but rather "using your willpower to look at things." You need to look at the world consciously and proactively.

3

The Starting Point of Right View

The gateway to the practice of self-reflection is how you look at others

I would like to explain more about this act of looking at, or observation. What are the points to consider when contemplating the act of observation?

The first point to think about at the start of self-reflection when observing is the appearance of others. This is the most accessible entry point.

One of the reasons people are prone to make mistakes, particularly mental mistakes, is that they do not understand others. Perhaps "not understanding" is not quite accurate; "not fully understanding" is more appropriate.

No matter how much you have observed someone, the true personal qualities of that person may not be so easy to value. Even if you have been a friend of the person for ten or twenty years, you may not fully see all of the person's qualities.

It is clear that we are seeing some part of the personality of the person in the images we perceive of them. It may not be clear what part we are looking at, but we are judging that person's personality only by his or her appearance to us. All of us, 7.7 billion people in this world, make judgments in this way.

It seems to be an irresponsible way to make judgements. I am sure you have never been held accountable for "how you saw others." Considering your past experiences, would you agree with that? You should hardly be held accountable for the way you see someone.

If you were held responsible, it would have been because of the way you talked about that person. This is an issue to be discussed later in the section on Right Speech. You may be held accountable by talking about or expressing something, but you are not held responsible only for seeing.

A source of misery lies in differences of understanding

I would like to point out that the appearance of a person or the world we are seeing may be likened to what can be captured by human eyes from many different angles.

You may know of the art style called Cubism, which expresses objects in a three-dimensional manner; it is as if they were being seen from different angles. I may not know the full meaning of the style, but I think Pablo Picasso wanted to reveal a different world as seen through spiritual eyes.

I believe Picasso's thoughts were: "I'm not satisfied with the two-dimensional flat images that people can usually see. The world created by God cannot be captured in a two-dimensional plane. It must be viewed in a more spiritual, presentative, and comprehensive manner." And the results of his efforts were displayed in the Cubist style in his art.

We see a lot of people, but we cannot always fully observe them from all angles. If you could understand every person completely, would it still be possible to have differences in understanding? What kind of confusion could possibly occur? What kind of misfortune might happen?

Isn't a root of misery a "difference in understanding?" The gap between "your understanding of yourself" and "other people's understanding of you," or between "your understanding of others" and "their perception of themselves," seems to have created hardships in human relationships.

When you think in this way, you will be challenged with a grave situation. It is possible that you would be afraid to open your eyes. Yet you are actually expected to have a sense of responsibility like this.

You might ask yourself if the image you see of people is really believable. You get an impression of a person through your eyes, but can you accept it as it is? Is the impression certain?

Whether they are aware or not of their importance, everyone makes evaluations of others based on the impressions they have of them. You are evaluating people based on your impression, but there is also the question of whether your judgment is adequate or not.

As you can see, the simple act of looking at people bears significant importance.

4

The Images of Yourself and of the Others Are Like Mirrors That Reflect Each Other

Just as it is difficult to "look at people all day in the right way," it is also hard to "look at yourself rightly." This is also an essential aspect of self-reflection.

People who cannot look at others rightly cannot look at themselves rightly either. In other words, people who are unable to see themselves cannot see others. Both are true.

Those who really do not know themselves cannot know others. It is the same as saying, "anyone who could not find God's child or Buddha's child in oneself cannot find it in others."

Also, people who are not able to recognize some aspect in others that is contrary to the mind of God or Buddha cannot see it in themselves. They cannot see themselves as being against the minds of God or Buddha, and as acting, behaving, or living accordingly.

Similarly, those who are not able to see the flaws in the way they live, in the eyes of God or Buddha, would have difficulty in finding such flaws in others. This is generally the case, though there are different degrees of misunderstanding.

"Looking at others" and "looking at yourself" are like viewing mirrors that reflect one another, and only when you can truly see both yourself and others can you see the true state of beings. Indeed, the self and the others are just like reflecting mirrors.

There is no one who can only see others but not oneself, nor anyone who only sees oneself but not others. Only when you are able to look at both can you see the real images of yourself and others or the true image of the world.

5

The Criteria for Looking at People Rightly

So, where should we focus on when thinking about "rightness" when looking at others and looking at ourselves? What should we carefully watch for when we take in what we see?

1) Observe objectively

Concerning the criteria to make assessments of others, it is important to first objectively take in the "appearance of others" as information.

You should not try to judge on the basis of your subjective values; instead, you should be careful to accept the information objectively. What kinds of personalities do people have? How do they act? How do they present themselves? What kinds of facial expressions do they have? You must first look at these objectively.

At this stage, it is important to be as selfless as possible. Set aside your own interest; focus on observation. Observation is the first step.

2) Recognize how you feel

Next is to consider how you feel about the person's appearance. After looking at someone objectively, recognize how you feel about it.

For instance, at first glance, you may feel that a person is good or bad. You may feel a certain person to be likable or not. Sometimes you may feel a person to be smart or the opposite.

You may find the person to be a little annoying or harsh. Sometimes you may feel a person to be kind or a bit naive.

There is a great variety of responsive feelings you may have, and you should be looking at this person with some kind of opinion. You need to know how you felt about the person you observed. This is the second step.

3) Look at the person from their point of view

The third step is to consider what the image of the other person would be if you were in the other person's position. You need to consider this measure of judging others.

For instance, if you found a certain person to be harsh or severe, how would you feel if that person commented on the impression you had about him or her? Would that person find your view to be fair? Would the person feel that your view is only partially right, or totally irrelevant?

In this way, you need to try to take into account other people's opinions.

Just by using this reasoning, you will realize that people will have different opinions of themselves than you have.

You may have a certain view of another person. While that person may agree with certain parts of your opinion, there may be disagreement with other parts of it. You may feel that the other person would surely hold a differing opinion. So you can see that there is much misalignment of perceptions.

At times both opinions may be exactly the same, or they may differ totally, or they may only share certain aspects. There will be many outcomes.

4) Observe in the context of Truth

The fourth thing to do after going through the three steps above is to consider the assessments from the standpoint of Truth. You have to determine which of the views is closer to the Truth, either your own analysis and feeling of the image of the other person, or the impression of the other person's image when taking his or her standpoint into account. You need to consider both views in the context of the Truth.

When gauging these assessments in the context of the Truth, you can make use of the knowledge of Truth you study daily. The accumulation of these studies of Truth is useful.

For instance, you need to consider what kind of opinion the high spirits would have of a certain type of person. Regarding your impression or opinion of the person, what sort of advice would high spirits give you? You need to think carefully about it.

If you have been able to read the spiritual messages of Jesus Christ I have published, then you could use his thoughts to contemplate your own view of another person. In your thinking about the other person, is there any room for adjustment?

Possibly you have read another of my books, *The Essence of Buddha*. Based on what is taught in the book there may be a number of factors to consider: You may have a certain image of yourself, but how would you appear to another person, and how would it measure from the standpoint of the Truth?

By referring to these other viewpoints of evaluation, you need to analyze how adequate your image of yourself is. How correct is the other person's image of you, at least what you assume to be the other person's image of you? If there is a difference between the two images, then how different, or to what degree is the other person's view of you more appropriate?

If you find there is a crucial gap between the images held by two parties as the result of careful review, then you need to make efforts to bring them into harmony. Self-reflection in its truest form involves this kind of effort.

5) Consider both your own and the other person's opinions as if in communication with God or Buddha

In the fourth step, I suggested looking at things rightly on the basis of Truth, but it can also be explained differently. You will find that the fourth step, observing something in the context of the Truth, or against your knowledge of the Truth, is already difficult. In this case, there is another method that can be followed.

What is it? I would say, "Leave behind all concerns and quietly examine your thoughts and those of the other person as though you were in communication with God." Let go of any interest or attachment, and observe the state of your being and that of the other person: Is there a possibility that the image you had of the person was wrong? Or, is the other person's self-image not totally correct? When you become aware of any difference in perception, then how would you fill the gap? You need to ask yourself this as you let go of any self-interest.

When you do this – even if the other person did not favorably impress you – you may find that you have made an incredible mistake in your assessment. You may find that the other person's standpoint was appropriate after all. You may find that the other person's objection to your assessment makes more sense.

6

Wisdom That Comes before Love

How to observe a person who is conceited and impertinent

When you look at people, you might use many different perspectives.

Perhaps a person has a tendency to become easily conceited. Actually, many among you are no exceptions to this tendency. For instance, you may be given an important role. At Happy Science, you may have passed an advanced seminar exam, or be appointed a branch manager or other leadership position. At this point, you may be seen as a qualified person. But that might change over time. One year later, a person may be different compared to the year before. There are three possibilities: The person has improved, has deteriorated, or is just maintaining the status quo.

With those possibilities in mind, suppose you are observing someone. That person may have become so conceited as to be on the verge of a tragic fall. In that situation, there are many different ways to look at the person.

In one way, you may think you need to scold the person as things are going very wrong.

However, there is another point of view. In addition to having to reprimand the person because of the mistakes he or she has made, there is still a viewpoint that you should reflect on, which is how you treated the person with love up until then.

So, ask yourself:

"Is the reason why he has become like that because of my overindulgence?

"Love involves kindness, but kindness may turn into indulgence. I may have led him into this dangerous situation as a result of letting him indulge in his own desires.

"Now, what needs to be taken into account is that the situation he is in is not only because of his own mistakes. Rather, there is the need to consider that I may have lacked wisdom before giving love. That may have resulted in this situation."

This is another possible viewpoint in looking at the situation.

Reflect on whether you had wisdom prior to giving love

Reflect on this:

"When giving love to him, if he had such a tendency that would cause risk, should I probably have looked ahead and modified the way I treated him?

"Or should I have probably guided him in a step-by-step manner, allowing him to grow gradually? Was there a possibility that I mistakenly thought that love was to give him anything he wanted?

"While the idea of giving love with one's bounty appears reasonable, if it is not yet time for him to advance, my act of giving love may have sprouted conceit within him.

"If so, even if I find great potential in him to eventually become eligible for a certain higher position, should I have been more perceptive of his personality? Then, as his awareness increased, could I have elevated his position, or entrusted him with more responsibilities in a step-by-step manner?"

In that way, there would be a type of self-reflection to see whether you have wisdom prior to giving love. Instead of simply thinking to reprimand a person for going astray, you should consider this possibility.

7

Beyond a Diversified Perspective

The more spiritually developed, the more diversified the perspective

As we have explored, there are quite a few ways to look at things. As you keep searching for more possibilities over time, your soul will progress. Your soul will make a leap forward. The very fact that you can look at things from many perspectives signifies the advancement of your spiritual level and personality. If you are only able to look at things one-sidedly, it means that your spiritual growth is still insufficient. The more you grow spiritually, the more you can see things from different angles.

This is surely the case concerning God or Buddha. He is able to view all things from every possible aspect, and then make applicable evaluations. Getting closer to His awareness means that you will gain the ability to look at things from several angles and understand diversified views. As you advance in the process of exploring the Truth, you will acquire diverse perspectives.

Upon acquiring diverse perspectives, you need to make judgments that are closer to the mind of God or Buddha

However, it is not enough just to hold diversified views. If you simply accept diversity and accept any opinion, saying, "This is one manner of observation, but there is also another way," as though you might display merchandise in a shop, virtually avoiding coming to a conclusion and making any judgment, this form of diversity does not produce any fruit. While diversified perspectives are necessary, if they only produce a variety of results leaving a problem unresolved, then this means that you have not made any spiritual effort. You need to know this.

It is clearly spiritual progress when you become able to look at things from a variety of perspectives. However, if you are able to hold diversified views that produce diversified conclusions, and you just leave them as they are, then it would just be anarchy. This would turn into chaos, and it would mean that the spiritual growth that has sprouted would wither.

Once you have achieved a diversified perspective, you must definitely make judgments that reflect the mind of God or Buddha. After having carefully considered many different ways of looking at things, you must reach your own best conclusion that your Buddha Nature, or divine nature, allows, based on your wholehearted spiritual effort. This should not be avoided.

If the result of your effort to achieve a diversified perspective in looking at things is an unsettled tolerance of all views because everyone has some good points, I would say that this is not acceptable. This would be the beginning of a world of chaos. Understanding is important, but meaning should be attached to the understanding. This is where your responsibility to attach meanings to situations arises.

8

Look at People with
a Blend of Generosity and Rigor

Learning the difficulty of looking at people rightly
from the end of Jesus' life

Responsibility comes with the final conclusion of whether you have looked at things rightly or not, and this takes courage. No matter who you are, it definitely takes courage.

Indeed, this happened for even the great figure called Jesus Christ. When he was finally crucified on Golgotha, he blessed the sinners nearby. He also said of the people who had caused him harm, "Father forgive them, for they know not what they do." When referring to this perspective of Jesus, it is quite difficult to judge how rightly he looked at things in his last moments; was it 100% right, 99.9% right, or 99% right?

In saying that, in consideration of his situation, surely he made nearly the best possible decision based on his own perspective. Some of his teachings were:

"If anyone slaps you on the right cheek, turn to him the other also."

"And if anyone would sue you and take your tunic, let him have your cloak as well."

"And if anyone forces you to go one mile, go with him two miles."

What was the result of practicing these ideas? They led to Jesus' tragic end.

His meaning was similar to the idea that, if there are those who intend to use violence, you should let them do so. We all know what resulted; Jesus' life was ended on the cross as he blessed the sinners and expressed love for those who persecuted him. His perspective at the end of life was certainly plausible. However, in considering the process that led to his tragic end, if asked whether he was looking at things rightly, I am afraid I cannot answer "Yes" in wholehearted agreement.

Regarding the way his observations, analysis, understanding, and feeling about things led to his final end, I cannot necessarily accept them as reasonable. There must have been reasons for and a set of circumstances resulting in his extreme situation. A comment on the final outcome would be: "In the process, couldn't he have had a better or higher perspective of looking at people?"

Judas' problem was also a tragedy caused by Jesus' generosity

Now we should think about the issue concerning Judas. It is a problem of how Jesus looked at Judas. This is also mentioned in the spiritual messages of Jesus Christ that I have published. It is about how Jesus saw Judas and his behavior, including how he thought about Judas' end.

Simply put, the question is, "Why did Jesus allow Judas to take such liberties?" If Jesus truly observed Judas in the right way, why did he let him have his own way? Why didn't he reprimand him before it was too late? Why didn't Jesus look after Judas more wisely? Why didn't he give more love based on wisdom? These are points to consider.

Jesus would have surely known about Judas' tendencies and from them could have foreseen the outcome. However, because he was one of the disciples whom Jesus once loved in the early days of the mission, and because he once worked so hard to support Jesus, it must have been difficult to treat Judas harshly.

In fact, Jesus was fully aware that Judas was starting to fall back spiritually, and that he was about to open a spiritual pathway from which evil spirits were frequently attempting to possess him. The other disciples were also not happy about Judas and actually asked Jesus to settle the matter. However, he hesitated to be too strict, considering the fact that Judas was one of his first disciples and had done much hard work in the beginning. Considering the love Judas had once dedicated, Jesus was reluctant to be sharp with him.

We all know the result of this. It is possible to say it was destiny. On the other hand, you could also say it was not really destined. There was still room for choice.

This means that even such a great Guiding Spirit like Jesus still had shortcomings in looking at things rightly, that even he was not able to achieve the ultimate level in his efforts. In his past lives, why did Jesus die many tragic deaths? It would be simple to say it was his fate, or it was the role he was assigned to play. You could also conclude that those outcomes occurred because Jesus thought the essence of love was self-sacrifice.

In his past incarnations, Jesus met with tragic deaths again and again. That was the case in his incarnation as Agasha, the great king of Atlantis. He also experienced similar dreadful deaths in other incarnations. As Agasha, events went as far as his execution to be buried alive. He let it happen. Agasha chose to let things happen rather than being forced to do so. It happened because of his own perspective of love. For love, the love of many people, he thought the greatest act of all was to sacrifice his own life.

I see this as one way to express love. However, because of his naivety and generosity, or because he let people go unchecked in their arrogance, tragedies occurred.

Shakyamuni Buddha was different from Jesus in looking at people

A contrasting figure was Shakyamuni Buddha. In his many past incarnations, there were hardly any in which he had ever been killed. Why is that?

It is because of the great difference between Jesus' and Shakyamuni's ways of looking at things. In the effort to bring out the greatest potential in people, the key is a combination of generosity and severity. This is indeed the most difficult thing to do. Similar to blending coffee beans of different varieties, the most difficult part of looking at people is to determine the particular blend of generosity and severity with which to treat a particular person. This blend will create a distinct "aroma."

9

Perspectives toward Surroundings

Can you see the world where you are allowed to live?

In considering whether you are looking at things rightly, another very important perspective is how you look at the world around you, in addition to allowing for the different perspectives between yourself and others.

In short, the question is whether you can see the world in which you are allowed to live. This may be explained as how you view the environment where you live. Very often the causes of happiness and misfortune depend on how you see the environment around you. Those who are studying our approaches at Happy Science should be well aware of this. You must have learned that the cause of happiness or misfortune depends on how we look at the environment around us, and that great emphasis is put on this point of view.

This is because there is no such thing as an ideal environment that is 100% complete. You may feel envious of a certain person's circumstances, but these circumstances may not necessarily be perfect when applied to you. Again, there is no such thing as the perfect environment.

For instance, if you are the kind of person who wishes to live a luxurious life, then living in a royal palace may be your dream life. However, for those who aspire to learn the Truth, living in a royal palace can cause suffering in a different sense. There is no such thing as a perfect, objective environment in which everything will result in satisfaction and give you absolute happiness.

"If your mind changes,
your environment will look different"
"You will see an environment that
corresponds to your own state of mind"

Now let me talk about two different perspectives concerning one's environment. The first perspective is that if your mind changes, your environment will look different. This is similar to the Buddhist idea that the three realms – the realm of desire, the realm of form, and the realm of non-form – are the reflection of the mind; this idea is relevant to some extent.

The other perspective is that you will see an environment that corresponds to your own state of mind. This is similar to the first perspective but slightly different. While the former calls for modifying the way you look at a given environment, the second perspective involves a change in the environment itself. That is the difference between the two perspectives of environment.

As you change your way of looking at things, one of two phenomena will apply. First, you may notice that your previous environment will appear to be different, or you will be given a new environment as a result of having changed your perspective. Both are true. There can be some time lag, but usually, the first phenomenon will take place, followed by the second.

Now, you should consider why happiness or misfortune occurs as the result of changing your perspective toward your environment. This conclusion will be mentioned in Chapter 4 on Right Speech.

10

Be Observant of Plants and Animals

Another important element of looking at things is keeping a watchful eye on animals, plants, and other non-human creatures. You should never forget about them. In considering animals, there are the common fish, cows, pigs, and bees, among other species. Have you ever thought of the benefits they give us? Probably most people have never considered this seriously. Images of animals pass through human sight in so many places, but people usually do not give a second thought to them. Their images do not register, and people just pass by.

If you consider this situation from the opposite standpoint, it would seem very cruel. Suppose you are an office worker; if your boss does not appreciate your hard work, you will surely be frustrated. Animals and plants work hard to fulfill roles. They provide beneficial goods and services to humans. Flowers are also making the utmost efforts to grow in order to create beautiful scenes to please us. Have you ever thought about that? Have you ever wondered why the beauty of flowers is enjoyable to our eyes, as flowers exert their life energy to the fullest?

When you become experienced in the True Eightfold Path, you will truly understand the feelings of plants. You will indeed understand them, as their feelings are conveyed to you, and you will see fully whether they are in a happy or sad state. You will eventually reach this level, understanding the feelings of animals, too. That is what you can expect.

Those who are unable to truly see the essence of various forms of life would never understand this. People who have not thought that these life forms make persistent efforts to live, or, to put it correctly, those who are not aware of their life struggle would never really understand their feelings. They would never have the emotion to sympathize with such creatures.

There is always a cause for an emotional change. Seeing is one of the most important causes of change. In order to create a proper, refined emotion, it is essential to look at things in a rightful way.

I have so far discussed Right View at the beginner's level, focusing faithfully on the literal meaning of "seeing" in relation to religious life. Those who have studied Buddhism deeply have sometimes explained Right View as "Right Faith," or "right viewpoint." "Right observation" is also another way to explain Right View. Right Faith is, of course, the foundation of Right View. Upon devoting oneself to faith, one is required to abandon one's past wrong faith, materialism, and theories of scientific positivism. Once you have become a believer, Right View is an important yardstick to give daily feedback of mental awareness.

Chapter 3

Right Thought

Lecture given on January 21, 1989
at Happy Science Training Hall, Tokyo

1

The Standard of Right Thought Is the Mind of God

Exploration of the Right Mind at Happy Science centers around Right Thought

From this chapter on, I will discuss the most important elements of the Eightfold Path. Right Thought is not so easy to master completely. No matter how many reincarnations you may go through, it will not be easy to achieve this discipline. I think you will understand that Exploration of the Right Mind at Happy Science centers around Right Thought, but it is not easy to achieve mastery of this.

First of all, what is the foundation of Right Thought? It is the mind of God or Buddha. No matter how much you think about or pursue Right Mind, it is not so easy to understand. I think this would actually apply to most people.

This is because the foundation of Right Mind is not supposed to be sought in humanity. It is what you seek in God or Buddha. The only place you can find the way to measure Right Mind is in God or Buddha, and nowhere else. It is the only place.

If God's mind was based on something else, human attitudes and patterns of behavior would accordingly become different.

However, the reason why human beings are obliged to go in a certain direction, as if following the polar star, is that Right Mind is defined from God's standpoint. That is how it can be understood.

El Cantare Consciousness at the root of Right Thought

So where should we seek the standard called Right Mind, which is determined by God? Let us think about this.

Other explanations of the Eightfold Path usually start from the standpoint of human beings, but here, let us think about it from a higher perspective.

Within the Earth Spirit Group exists the ninth-dimensional Cosmic Realm where the saviors abide. Beneath it are several realms: the eighth dimension, the seventh dimension, and so on, that correspond to the states of attainment for all souls.

In the ninth dimension, there exist ten Great Spirits centering around the El Cantare Consciousness. El Cantare is the head of the Earth Spirit Group, and decisions are made under His leadership.

So, when we are exploring Right Mind, or pursuing Right Thought, the El Cantare Consciousness is most relevant.

El Cantare has the quality of both the Mahavairocana Buddha (Buddha as the Dharma-body) and the Great Savior. In short, El Cantare is the great spiritual being that unites Buddha and God.

The name El Cantare has not previously been made known on earth, and the existence called "El Cantare" is actually the

God of the Earth. This being was referred to as "heavenly father" by Jesus Christ, "Allah" in Islamic belief, "Ame-no-Mioya-Gami" in Japanese Shinto, and the "emperor in heaven" in China. It is the embodiment of immense Light that radiates spiritual light on the entire Earth Spirit Group.

Traditionally, there has been faith in Mahavairocana, but it has actually been faith in the existence called El Cantare. In past history, His existence has previously not been clearly explained, but His existence is real.

This fact has never been revealed before because the core consciousness of El Cantare has only incarnated twice before in the history of the Earth Spirit Group. However, branch spirits of El Cantare have incarnated many times before on earth to guide humankind. Consequently, His existence has been previously presumed in different ways.

Now He has descended to earth for the third time in the present, and clearly has revealed His name, "El Cantare."

2

Integrating Diverse Teachings

The reason Happy Science introduces opinions of a variety of spirits

Until now, I have published a variety of spiritual messages and interviews, introducing the thoughts of numerous consciousnesses including Bodhisattvas and Tathagatas. I believe many of you have studied them. However, if these ideas were left as just a diverse set of teachings, human beings would not know in which direction to head for.

One of the reasons why I have introduced the opinions of spirits from various levels at Happy Science is to show the wide range of characters of the spirits. In this sense, I will continue to introduce different opinions of spiritual beings to show their diversity.

One problem, however, is that even high spirits from the eighth or ninth dimensions can have different opinions, making it difficult for people on earth to assimilate them to form their own views. Some people may simply decide that "Any opinion is fine," but that would be a somewhat dangerous way of thinking from the perspective of Right Thought.

The limitation of people on earth who cannot discern the different levels of consciousnesses as if they were all spread on a flat plane

So what is wrong with this way of thinking? It is necessary to consider this. Why is there a problem if the diversity is left as it is, and how can diversity be correctly understood? It is necessary to know more about this matter. When it comes to why the teachings and ideas of spiritual beings appear to be so diverse, it is because they are recognized by my consciousness.

I can comment on what other saviors or high spirits like Tathagatas and Bodhisattvas are trying to say to convey their teachings. Moreover, I can explain the different levels of these consciousnesses. It is actually my mission to teach them. But what would happen if people on earth take those opinions and just try to emulate them without fully knowing the differences in the spiritual levels? From the earthly viewpoint, the differences cannot be recognized, and therefore all opinions appear as plain alternatives. They only appear as optional differences of consciousness that are spread out flatly before them.

I know clearly that there are differences between the consciousnesses not only from a horizontal aspect, but also from the vertical and depth perspectives. Therefore, I can tell you where a specific spiritual being's idea can be placed on the coordinate axes of the Spirit World measured by the vertical, horizontal, and depth perspectives.

In contrast, people usually see the differences in a two-dimensional perspective. So one would assign a certain spiritual view at a point somewhere on a plane from where one is sitting or standing. In other words, there is a tendency to consider the different opinions of high spirits as similar to the difference in opinion between oneself and someone with a different mindset. This means that you are interpreting the coordinate axes of the multiple dimensions above this three-dimensional world as two-dimensional or flat. You need to know the meaning of the difference in the manner of interpretation. If you make a mistake here, you will never achieve Right Thought. This is a very essential point.

The Laws of El Cantare that integrate various teachings

Consequently, for the next level of awareness, it is necessary to integrate the variety of ideas. Unless taught in this way, people cannot possibly understand, and this will cause confusion.

The Consciousness working on their integration is El Cantare. I am now focusing on teaching the Laws of El Cantare in order to integrate ideas on the levels below the ninth dimension.

I will continue to publish spiritual messages and interviews but will also work to integrate the different thoughts under the ideas of the consciousness that exists at a higher level. In this way, different ideas are becoming integrated.

3

The Meaning of Diversity

Faith is the key to know the world of God or Buddha

Now, why does the being of a higher level intend to integrate different opinions? It is a question of faith.

What is faith? It is the power to know the world of God. Without faith, you cannot understand this world. Faith is the key to knowing the world of God or Buddha.

Faith can also be expressed as being open to the ideas of those with higher awareness. "The spirit of humbly learning the intentions and thoughts of those who are at higher levels" is called faith.

Without this attitude, the different ideas from various higher levels would be translated only as if they existed on the same level. Consequently, the different ideas of higher beings would only be understood in the same way the different ideas among people on earth are viewed. It would be because of people's inability to assess the relative value of the higher beings' opinions and where they can be placed, and this would be dangerous.

I had sensed such a danger previously, as I published various spiritual messages. Because people were unable to determine the correct spiritual position of what I taught from the perspective of a higher dimension, they tended to take the teachings from a mistaken viewpoint and interpret them differently.

Therefore, I intend to compile what I have already published from the perspective of the higher dimensions. Otherwise, people cannot understand. From my standpoint, I have a clear overview of the other spirits' teachings; however, from the perspective of human beings on earth, it is not necessarily visible. Please do not mistake this.

The meaning of the "diversity" embodied in the Light of God, and cautionary comments

What is the next thing that matters?

The Light coming from above flows through a prism and is divided into seven colors to shine over the Spirit World and the world on earth. Various ideologies are embodied in the various colors on the spectrum of Light. To make it easier for human beings to understand, certain ideas can sometimes be expressed as the "teaching of love," the "teaching of mercy," the "teaching of courage," or the "teaching of wisdom." In this way, quite a variety of teachings have been taught.

Light has thus been divided by a prism to facilitate the process of learning for human beings. And each soul can start learning what is most suitable for oneself.

Consequently, each soul experiences spiritual discipline expressed in a ray of certain color, such as yellow, blue, or purple, but it is necessary to bear in mind that this arrangement is just a process for each soul's spiritual evolution. Suppose that your learning was from within the purple ray of Light; in such a case, you must not claim that only the purple ray is truthful. Instead, you must accept that other people who are learning under different colors of Light, such as red or yellow, are also good.

So you can see that the diversity of teachings is basically a way for people in training to develop tolerance allowing them to acknowledge each other while mutually keeping a distance. Diversity does not mean that people who have experienced spiritual discipline through a certain path should harbor antagonism for people of other disciplines, but is rather meant to prove that together these people can live to create the great art of God.

However, this does not mean that God's teaching can just be a choice of just anything, from A, B, C, or D. If you are not able to firmly grasp this point, you will never know what Right Thought is. If this diversity is misinterpreted, and you determine that the teaching A, the teaching B, and the teaching C are all equally positive, then Right Thought in the Eightfold Path does not make sense. If you think that people can choose any way of spiritual discipline to please themselves, then Right Thought cannot be a target to pursue. Then, Exploration of the Right Mind in Happy Science would be meaningless.

Therefore, we must not forget that there is one ultimate source of everything. Each teaching that has branched out from the single source is presented as a school of learning to match the tendency of each soul and the progress of their spiritual discipline.

Being part of a certain path that has split from the original source, one thing you need to be careful about is this: You must not think your way of thinking is absolute. You must have a heart of tolerance to respect others who belong to different paths and learn from them.

4

Building Consensus in the Heavenly World

Accepting the existence of the world created by God that goes beyond your perception

In Chapter 1 of this book, I stated that the steps of "exploration, study, and missionary work" are based on faith in a broad sense.

It is not about exploration in the context of natural science. It is not an investigation in the scientific sense, accepting an idea if an experiment proves it to be "positive," or rejecting it if it was proven to be "negative."

It is a solemn fact that the world created by God exists, whether human beings explore it or not. Equally, the laws that govern this world absolutely exist. They exist whether human beings see them or not, hear them or not. This is the premise, and those who do not understand this will never pass through the gateway of exploration.

If you think that exploring is only understanding what you can see through your physical eyes, your attempt to explore in this way can be extremely challenging. It would be similar to trying to see the universe through a microscope. Or it would be just like looking at the universe through a kaleidoscope. Please think about the vast difference in the manner of looking at things.

A group of 500 high spirits is giving guidance to Happy Science

The group of spiritual beings giving guidance to Happy Science is very large, consisting of approximately 500 high spirits. Never before has such a large number of spiritual beings come together to initiate a movement on earth. In a sense, it is also a new experience for the spirits in the heavenly world. Another interesting point is that high spirits who had no previous association with each other in the heavenly world are now interacting through their engagement in the activities of Happy Science.

In cases where there were initially some differences of opinion within the group of guiding spirits, the mainstream opinions within the group have become aligned together. Ever since the time the high spirits were quickly brought together, they have gradually come to an accord. This is because it became necessary to establish their unity in collective consciousness as the movement of Happy Science became full-fledged. People on earth will be confused unless they are pointed in a certain direction, so a consensus has been gradually built in the heavenly world, with El Cantare as the center. And many spiritual beings have been working together in order to realize united thinking on earth.

Therefore, my power will surely become greater and greater.

Exploration of the Right Mind has even greater significance, but if you focus on Right Thought in the Eightfold Path, you should never forget the viewpoint that at its foundation is the mind of

God or Buddha. You cannot start from your own way. You should not make that mistake.

5

Three Attitudes That Are Required for Right Thought

Now, what is needed to have Right Mind, which is in accord with the mind of God or Buddha? The next challenge is to explore this question. One must hold three basic attitudes to stand at the gateway of this challenge.

1) Being open-minded

The first attitude is to be open-minded.

If you wish to receive teaching from higher dimensions, it is impossible without being obedient and open to ideas. Otherwise, the teaching will pass you by, or the Light will be refracted without being taken in.

Even if you possess a certain rank, status, education, or appearance while living in this world on earth, you cannot possibly measure the world based on your ideas alone after becoming aware of the fact that what you base your pride on is akin to a small speck in this great universe that God created. Do not forget this premise.

Therefore, in order to understand this world that God created and His intentions, being obedient and open-minded is essential. This is the first attitude.

2) Self-help efforts

The second attitude required is the attitude of self-help.

I have been emphasizing the importance of "self-power," but I now feel this concept can easily mislead people. In other words, depending on your interpretation, it can easily cause mistakes. If we take self-power to mean egoistic power, then there is absolutely no possibility to approach the world of God or Buddha. It would mean that the people living in this three-dimensional world on earth could do anything they desired, so there would be no need for exploration or studying the Truth at all. Therefore, the term "self-power" should be replaced with "self-help efforts."

Moreover, there is no such idea as faith in self-power, in contrast to faith in other power. Self-power refers to one's approach to and attitude toward spiritual discipline, not having faith in it. I hope you do not make a mistake about this.

The difference between self-power and other power can simply be explained as the difference in the methodology within a spiritual discipline, whether you take up self-help efforts or think that such an attitude is troublesome, then ignore such efforts and immerse yourself completely in something greater. I would like to put emphasis on self-help efforts in Happy Science.

3) Being humble

The third attitude of importance is to be humble. This is somewhat related to having an open mind.

Enlightenment is to be achieved in steps. As you make advancement up the steps, without humility, you are likely to experience difficulty in receiving the Light. If you develop a feeling that you are somehow special as you progress, then this very notion will block the Light from reaching you.

What is this sense of being special? It is very similar to what is called pride or self-respect. Or, to express it in negative terms, you might call it conceit or satisfaction over minor success. This is the next barrier that is very difficult to surmount.

Even if you begin with an open mind and move up the steps toward enlightenment with the spirit of self-help, you may likely experience a period when your ego gradually gets bloated and you become conceited. Here, you need to renew your pursuit of humility.

These three attitudes are essential for you to enter into the world of Buddha's Truth.

6

Three Elements to Examine
in Relation to Right Thought

In seeking Right Thought, you should examine your thoughts according to the three attitudes mentioned in the previous section.

It is quite difficult to verify what are rightful thoughts against a specific checklist. However, as I discussed earlier, the three attitudes of being open-minded, making self-help efforts, and being humble are necessary in order to advance toward God or Buddha. So you may consider any thoughts that go against these attitudes obstructions to Right Thought.

1) What prevents you from being open-minded
– the shell of ego

Now, what would hinder the attitude of "being open-minded" that was first mentioned? We need to think about what would obstruct an open-minded approach to accept the Truth, study it, and improve oneself.

It could be the "shell" that you have come to form around yourself over the past decades in the course of your life. This is to say that a "shell of ego" hinders openness. As you develop a certain way of living that you consider to be good and correct, a barrier-like shell forms to enclose you within a certain framework. This shell prevents you from being open-minded.

Therefore, you must first examine whether you have formed a kind of shell resulting from your particular way of sensing or seeing things, or in living your life. This is also a very important point to consider in self-reflection.

If you look over how you have lived in the past, you probably have certain traits that stand out and are different from the traits of others. Such differences have both positive and negative aspects. In any case, you can consider that the existence of such unique traits largely contributed to form a kind of shell around your mental attitude and lifestyle.

So when you reflect on your past, the first thing you can do is look at what has stood out the most in your life over the past thirty, forty, fifty, or sixty years, compared to other people.

As you consider the most outstanding traits that differentiate you from others, and how the way in which you have lived has led you in a certain direction, there will always be something you can think of. If you have experienced a life that included negative elements, even if you overcame them on your own, there will be some factor that still affects you.

Let us think about some examples.

Being physically disabled

Let us take the case of a physical disability. Some of you may have a physical disability that makes life more difficult compared to able-bodied people. You may have worked hard to overcome it, or still struggle with it. In any case, there is no doubt that your circumstance has caused you to form some form of shell in the process of your struggle. This is one example.

Being raised in either an extremely rich or poor family

Another example is the shell that is formed as a result of being raised in an extremely well-to-do-family. If you are born in a prestigious family, from highly respected parents, or in an extremely wealthy family, it can cause you to develop a certain form of shell.

On the contrary, there is another kind of shell that is caused by poverty. We are talking about the kind of shell that is caused by experiencing extreme poverty and being mentally trapped by the circumstances it entails.

Experiencing misfortune in the immediate family

Another example is an unfortunate circumstance in your family occurring in your childhood. You may have lost one or both of your parents. They may have divorced or remarried. You may have experienced some kind of family issue, and it would have surely affected you in some way.

Being conspicuous due to talent, study, education, or other ability

The same is true in terms of talent. If you have some prominent talent, there are probably both advantages and disadvantages that come with it.

Take the example of those who stand out in scholastic achievement; this has both positive and negative aspects. On the positive side, they can take advantage of their abilities to become involved in the knowledge industry or do intellectual activities, but on the other hand, they may have some troubles with human relationships. They may develop shy and withdrawn characters, becoming the type of people who are suspicious, focused on the negative traits of others, or just antisocial.

On the other hand, some people may struggle with poor school achievement. Some of these people may live with an inferiority complex, while others work hard to try to overcome their shortcoming, and even boast about it. In any case, some sort of shell is formed.

Therefore, in order to find your true self, you must first recognize the shell you have formed.

Do not use your own circumstances as excuses

To become open-minded, you need to remove the shell of your own making. You cannot face God or Buddha as a truthful person when you use the issues you have experienced due to your special circumstances as an excuse. As long as you keep making excuses, using your special circumstances to explain your behavior, you will never be open-minded. You could never achieve a truthful state of mind. You should first filter out your own special circumstances and related excuses. Without doing this, you will never be able to "think rightly."

So first of all, it is essential to remove the shell that each person has. Whether it is positive or negative, you need to remove any trace of the shell that had affected you and think again about yourself as an open-minded and pure human being. Unless you go through this process, you will never know your true self.

2) What interferes with self-help efforts – blaming other people or your circumstances for your misfortune

Do you blame others or your circumstances for your misfortunes?

The second thing that is essential in considering Right Thought is your attitude in making self-help efforts. Understanding the necessity of this kind of attitude depends on whether you acknowledge the reality that the world and universe that God has created is constantly evolving.

If you do not accept this reality, the minimum effect is that you will be left behind, and you may become a nuisance to others who are about to grow and develop.

Because the thoughts of God or Buddha include the desire for the evolution and development of everything, and as long as human beings are His children, we are all destined to grow.

Therefore, the next factor to examine in relation to Right Thought is the very attitude of self-help efforts: Do you have the aspiration to carry out self-help efforts toward growth? Or on the contrary, do you always blame your circumstances or others for not advancing? You need to examine yourself in this way.

One of the most important things regarding Right Thought in the Eightfold Path is to realize that it is you who blames the circumstances and others for your failure to grow.

You must face up to this facet of yourself. Without confronting this, you can never practice self-reflection. This kind of cowardly emotion must be cast off. As long as you blame your circumstances, or what someone else has done, or issues in your workplace for your misfortune, you will never achieve anything.

As I have consistently pointed out, you should never think that your happiness or misfortune are determined by the two external factors of "other people" and "surrounding circumstances." Anyone who has read my previous books or heard my lectures must be familiar with this. I have repeatedly stated that before blaming these two outside factors, you should reflect deeply on yourself.

"Your current state is the result of what you have previously decided and chosen. As a person suffering from 'unhappiness syndrome,' you have probably made negative decisions in the past."

"Even if people are placed in similar environments, experience the same conditions, or suffer the same problems, their individual ways of living would be different depending on the person."

This is what I have been teaching.

Human beings are not like *pachinko* balls or billiard balls. They do not always follow the physical laws. Under the same conditions, even if an equal power is exerted in the same direction, the outcome differs from person to person. Given the same situation, some will become happy, while others become unhappy. There is no one but yourself who brings about the results. It is your mind.

I would like you to understand that without such a mindset there would be no basis for Happy Science in the first place. If you can achieve happiness in your life blaming your circumstances and others for any shortcomings, then there would be no foundation for Happy Science. There would be no such effort as Exploration of the Right Mind or any methodology for the scientific study of happiness. I would like you to understand this.

"The awareness of responsibility" will break down the barrier of pride to set a starting point for self-help efforts

It all starts from doing away with a mindset that contradicts the spirit of self-help efforts, denying the tendency to easily blame others and surrounding circumstances. Rather, you should take responsibility for your current situation. Taking a sense of responsibility will be the driving force behind your self-help efforts. When you take full responsibility for your own state of mind or your present surroundings, you will be motivated to overcome whatever problem that causes you unhappiness and stand on your own feet.

However, if you think your problem is the fault of someone or something else – your parents, your circumstances, your friends or colleagues, your poverty in childhood or your current lack of money or even the bad weather – you will never get better.

Indeed, the starting point for self-help efforts is to have a sense of responsibility. It is a willingness to take responsibility for your life. Those who cannot do this tend to try to protect themselves. This is called "pride," but this thick barrier of pride blocks the Light of

God or Buddha and prevents people from practicing self-reflection. The way to break through this barrier of pride is to foster a sense of responsibility, or the attitude of taking responsibility for your own life.

People are prone to evade responsibility. It is a weakness of human beings to seek an easy way out to escape responsibility, not only for the misfortunes of others but also for their own misfortunes. You may naturally want to evade liability for the misfortunes of others, but also tend to try to escape from being liable for your own bad situation.

Nevertheless, you can only progress after accepting your responsibility. Your improvement starts from this acceptance.

Surely, circumstances or other people may cause you unhappiness, but it is your own problem as you have invited the situation to take place. It is your responsibility to face it, and that is where the path to happiness begins.

Only after accepting your responsibility is there room for you to make efforts. And as a result of your self-help efforts, you can expect improvements to come. Never forget this.

In particular, if you are members of Happy Science, I would like you to be aware of your responsibility. Instead of blaming others, accept your own responsibility. Then what would become of it? This is the next challenge.

3) What prevents you from being humble – jealousy and the desire for self-display

Do you give blessings for the happiness of others?

Now, let us think about what would prevent humility, the third important point for Right Thought.

What happens when humility is lost? This means that one is not satisfied unless one is always the "boss."

What are the characteristics of such a domineering personality type? First of all, such people tend to think that there is nothing to learn from others. They will also seek to rationalize and justify their own standing. What happens as a result is the abandonment of their willingness to make progress. Instead, they will start seeking ways to bring down or remove others who they feel stand in their way.

Here is one important truth that I would like to draw your attention to: You will be ruined if you lose the spirit to celebrate the happiness of others. You should remember that I have said this.

If you were truly humble, you would be able to celebrate other people's happiness, but the more arrogant you were, the less easy it would be for you to honor the joy of others. You would feel that the enjoyment of happiness is allowed only for you, and you would hate for others to enjoy happiness.

What follows next is that you would start to interfere with someone else's happiness. You may do this either intentionally or unconsciously.

The True Eightfold Path

If you intentionally interfere with others at work, for example, you may purposely deceive your colleagues, ruin their efforts, tell on them to a supervisor, or mislead their subordinates.

If you are unconsciously doing so, you would often explain your actions using your beliefs. You tend to force others to follow the beliefs you have formed in the course of your life. You have most likely experienced both happiness and unhappiness in your life until now, but you will advance your version of thinking and pressure others into accepting it. This is an unconscious way of interference.

These are two typical ways of interfering with the happiness of other people.

People who achieved success through hardships tend to enforce their beliefs on others, with the intention of obstructing the advantaged

Let us look at the example of a founder and president of a company. He struggled greatly as he worked his way up, and now cannot bear those who seem to have advanced without hardship. The founder toiled hard to create and manage his company, growing it gradually from a small business into a large corporation employing thousands or tens of thousands of workers. At that point, many candidates considered "elite" would likely seek employment there.

This is where the founder unconsciously starts to impose his own beliefs by manifesting his "credo" to his employees. These could

· 98 ·

be beliefs such as "People can never grasp the truth or do a good job unless they work their way up from the bottom." Thinking in this way, the founder gradually chooses to refuse those who seem to have been well-bred. He cannot tolerate those who seem to advance effortlessly and smoothly.

Konosuke Matsushita, the founder of Panasonic, did exactly the opposite. He had almost no education, had poor health, and went through a lot of hardships, but he accepted his circumstances as they were and respected the abilities of his subordinates, regarding them as better than himself. He would ask his subordinates for help when he felt his abilities were inadequate. Mr. Matsushita believed that his company would naturally grow because he had such a competent team.

This is a notable example of a self-made man who never imposed his beliefs on others, but rather chose to leverage his disadvantages to achieve success.

However, his case is exceptional and would usually be difficult to emulate. Those who started from a small business and worked their way up are prone to start bullying other workers at some point. They tend to bully those who seem to have advanced without suffering. They may not be aware of such actions, but this behavior can manifest itself from their subconscious.

The issue of jealous women wanting to
disturb the happiness of colleagues

Please forgive me if I offend any of you, but some unmarried women or those women with long careers may also be acting similarly from their subconscious feelings. Of course, I know that many women can be very capable and kind at the same time, but some unconsciously obstruct the happiness of younger colleagues. Sometimes, they may interfere with younger women as they are being courted, or occasionally behave harshly toward younger men.

When hindering younger women being courted, the older women may make intimidating remarks that they "are flirting," "wearing inappropriate makeup," or "are not serious enough and consider their work to be temporary jobs." They may also abuse younger men to hamper their actions, claiming that they "are just chasing after girls instead of doing proper work." These are all examples of behaviors initiated from the subconscious level; they are attempts by people to obstruct someone else's happiness.

All these behaviors are done by people to justify themselves and their pride. These actions are also carried out without people realizing that they are living with the loving benevolence of God or Buddha and a great many others.

They crave more love, and when they see others receiving love, it is intolerable to them. They will then act, either on purpose or subconsciously, to bring down those who seem to be advantaged.

The feelings motivating this kind of behavior are also part of what we need to examine in relation to Right Thought. These are feelings expressed by words such as "jealousy," "grudge," "envy," or "resentment."

You must never forget that human beings are living in the light of the sun. The light of the sun shines over both good and bad people. Whether darnel weeds or wheat, the sun shines light on all plants.

Although the light of the sun is generously given to all beings, some people wish more of it to shine on themselves, like being in a spotlight.

Self-display is used to justify one's own way of life but deprives others of peace of mind and love

There is also the question of the desire to show off to impress others. The most important issue in considering humility is the desire for self-display.

To fight against this desire is also extremely difficult. The motivation behind the desire to be in the spotlight is to justify one's own way of life. This will lead to the desire to show oneself off.

The reason why the desire for self-display is not acceptable is that it takes away the peace of mind of others. It is also an attempt to divert the flow of love to oneself, even when it is intended for others.

This kind of person cannot stand the fact that sun shines equally on others. The desire for self-display is like thinking, "The light of the sun should only shine on my flowerpot."

The jealousy of others nearby restrains
the desire for self-display

Among the points to examine in relation to Right Thought is jealousy, which also has the effect of keeping the desire for self-display in certain people in check. In spite of the negative aspect of jealousy, it can still work in a positive manner.

That is, those who pursue their desire to show off will inevitably face the jealousy of other people. Consequently, the position of each person will be adjusted by the restraining effect of jealousy. The jealousy of others makes it difficult to carry out the desire for excessive self-display. This could be considered some kind of balancing effect.

However, jealousy by itself does not involve the giving of love, and expressing too much of it would give rise to evil, as it is just the reverse side of self-love.

Examine "wrong thoughts" one by one against the criteria of Right Thought

I have so far considered Right Thought based on a number of criteria.

As you can see, the criteria to examine thoughts to determine whether they are right involve a variety of factors. The standard way is to check each of the negative thoughts individually, starting from examining one's own complaining, frustration, and desire without moderation.

To make it easy to understand Right Thought, I have presented an organized way centering on the three main criteria of "being open-minded," making "self-help efforts," and "being humble." I believe these would make it very easy to check against Right Mind and determine whether you are thinking in a right way. I recommend you make it a regular practice to check against these criteria.

The above is a modern, easy-to-understand description of the practice of Right Thought. Considering traditional Buddhist learnings, the practice of Right Thought centers on self-reflection on greed, anger, and ignorance, which are collectively expressed as the "Three Poisons of the Mind." At a more advanced level, it is recommended that you examine your thoughts when meditating on the Six Worldly Delusions, which include conceit, doubt, and false views, along with the above three poisons. "Greed" is to want with no end; "anger" is the feeling of outrage; and "ignorance" is the lack of Truth. "Conceit" is egotism, or arrogance; "doubt" is thinking influenced by any corrupt media, or scientific thinking based on materialism and atheism; and "false views" are a wide range of wrong thoughts, in terms of religious beliefs, morality, or common sense, that should be completely done away with.

Chapter 4

Right Speech

正

語

Lecture given on January 7, 1989
at Happy Science Training Hall, Tokyo

1

The Influence of Words

Words spoken out loud will create
happiness or misfortune for yourself and others

Next, I would like to cover the topic of Right Speech. This, along with Right View, is a very important goal of spiritual discipline. However, Right Speech may not be easily achieved. I think that everyone who examines their mind based on the teachings of the Eightfold Path would sense this difficulty.

Imagine that everything you have said during the day was recorded; if the recording were played back before you went to bed, how would you feel? This is the first step in considering the practice of Right Speech.

"Imagine that at the end of a day, all the things you have said during the day were recorded and you must listen to the recording before going to sleep. How would you judge the content? Review what you have said during the day from someone else's eyes, or the standpoint of a third party."

This is what you are expected to do, and it would be extremely difficult. Attaining Right View is difficult, but Right Speech is even more difficult to achieve.

What would be the impact of what you said on other people? What would be the influence of your spoken words on yourself? How are you affected by the words you say out loud? Most people would not be able to answer, and this would describe more than 90% of people. However, the words you say out loud would often be the very cause of your misfortune.

If you are a devotee of Happy Science, you may have been asked to give advice on various personal problems. People may confide in you, complaining, "I'm being abused," "My boss always scolds me," "My husband regularly uses physical violence on me," or "My wife constantly nags me with abusive language, and I'm suffering all the time." However, if you ask them to consider whether their problems actually bother them "all the time," the reality would be somewhat different.

"The boss who is always mad at you" may have only reprimanded you twice in a year. "The wife who grumbles all day long, from morning until late at night in bed," may only be complaining less than thirty minutes a day when really timed with a clock. Cases like these are quite common. However, those who suffer tend to feel the harmful words circling in their minds continuously.

Why does this happen? In many cases, those who suffer from verbal comments have a tendency to confirm what they have heard by speaking out loud about it. When they say something like, "You keep complaining all day long. Listening to your words is really making me ill," this perception becomes substance. Then, the husband becomes verbally bound by his own comment. Once it has been said out loud, it does not matter if his wife does not vocally hound him day after day. He feels he has to suffer. Because he said it himself, he believes in it, and it becomes materialized. Things like this happen very often.

Unless you try to register it in your mind, what happened on one day can be forgotten the next. However, if you express the thought in words, then it will remain in your mind and in the minds of others.

Words can cause love to help better the world, but they can also cause violence that destroys the world

Do the words of others remain in your mind, even though they were said five or ten years ago? The words that stick deep in your memory are often those spoken years ago. A casual phrase from someone can often remain in your memory and may continue to hurt you like a thorn in the flesh. On the other hand, the person who uttered the words may hardly remember doing so. Probably less than a tenth of people would remember things they said. If a more rigorous count were made, the number would probably be 2 or 3%.

The other person may not have been feeling well, or may have been in a bad mood or busy with other matters, and casually said something nasty. However, once said out loud, the words would remain in the minds of those who heard them. If someone heard what you said and the words became etched in their minds, they would endure. Of course, if the person is practicing self-discipline and has learned to let go of abusive words, it would be a different story. But ordinary people allow these words to persistently remain in their memories.

This is especially the case for women, who are more prone to be deeply affected by negative words. The stinging words they heard remain vividly imprinted in their memories, making them feel as if the words were just said. Even if the remarks were made a decade ago, as soon as they see the person who said them, the words automatically become alive again.

For instance, suppose ten years ago a man said to a woman, "I don't like you." He may like her now, but the moment she sees him, that memory from the past is replayed instantly. The statement would play across her mind as if on an electronic signboard. Even if he previously told her, "You have bad taste in fashion," he may have since changed his opinion, thinking better of her fashion sense. However, unless he said so aloud, the comment he made ten years ago would remain in her memory, and the moment she meets him, the bad memory will immediately light up. The impact of words has such an effect.

In Chapter 2, which concerns Right View, I mentioned that you are not held responsible for what you see; therefore, it is hard to judge the act of looking at things. In contrast, what you say can be examined objectively by those around you. The effect of speaking out loud can not only turn into love to create a better world; it can also turn into violence that can destroy the world.

2

Careless Words That Hurt Yourself and Others

There is no end to the pursuit of speaking rightly

You need to have courage to continue your efforts to speak better. It is a struggle, a fight against yourself.

The pursuit of "speaking right" has no end. There is no end to it, forever. The least you can do is aim to have a good night's sleep, even after hearing what you have said during the day. At the end of the day, after recalling what you have said, there might be so much regret as to cause you to have a sleepless night; this would be a big problem. If you could have peaceful sleep, being satisfied with having said fairly good things during the day, it would be fine. It is the least you can do in your efforts to achieve this state of mind.

Now, let me talk about the problem of causing deep hurt to someone with your words. If you had said things that hurt another person so much that your words remained in that person's mind for a long time, for years or even decades, then most often you will regret having said such things. It is likely you will feel regret right after having spoken the abusive words, or maybe the following day, or perhaps more than a week afterward. However, the problem is that most people cannot admit they were wrong, to say out loud that they have repented and have changed their attitude. Sadly, more than 90% of people are like this.

If you make a mistake when entering an accounting transaction on your computer, you need to make a correction entry to cancel the error. If the adjustment is not done correctly, you will have to cancel the correction and re-enter the right figure. This would be a troublesome task.

Similarly, if you think you have put something wrong into the mind of another person, you have to offset that with something good. Otherwise, the balance will always remain negative, and you cannot expect to have a good relationship. You have to work hard to make amends for what you did wrong to the other person.

Check to see if you may have hurt others or offended them with careless words

Pride is often the source of one's suffering. Many people might think that they are not liked by others. Do you think you are disliked by others? Or do you think others like you?

If you think that others dislike you, please make a careful self-analysis. If you think someone hates you, usually it is because of the words you speak. With few exceptions, the usual reason you are not liked by other people is because of what you say. Careless words you happen to say cause you to be shunned by others. One mistake might be excused, but if you keep repeating unpleasant things twice, three times, four times, and even more, people will no longer forgive you. At this point, people's perceptions of you will become fixed. They will judge you as someone who says unpleasant things and thinks in a certain way. Based on that viewpoint, you will be labeled as such.

Those who think they are disliked are those who have said things that hurt others. They have actually hurt others by offending their feelings. Even worse, they have not taken any action to offset the harm they caused. You might think, "Everyone treats me wrong and is antagonistic to me," but it is often because of a casual remark you made that irresponsibly irritated other people.

If that is the case, you can apologize to them, admitting, "I was really wrong in that situation," and your sense of wrongdoing will be relieved in a short while. Not many people are so ruthless as to continue punishing a person who apologizes. It would be a difficult thing to do. There would be reluctance to hurt or judge people who express regret.

3

Set Aside Your Pride and Do Not Be Afraid to Apologize

Angels enjoy seeing those who are self-reflecting, while devils are repelled

One of the noblest sights in the heavenly world is that of someone in self-reflection. When looking at those who reflect on their past and shed tears of regret, angels are joyous, and devils are no longer able to cause them any harm. Devils cannot approach people seen to be repenting in tears, nor can they tempt those people. Those who are truly sorry are immune to the devils' influence.

If you think you have suffered for a long time, it may simply be because of your pride. You might think, "My boss keeps bullying me," but the facts may be completely different. You may not be listening to what your boss says, or you act rebelliously all the time, or you simply do not do your job. You may only be rationalizing your behavior. If you change your attitude and apologize, that might solve the problems, but instead, you keep suffering from an "eternal hell" of your own making. There are so many stories like this.

This is often the situation of the spirits from hell. They strongly insist, "I refuse to repent," or "I definitely will not admit it was my mistake," or "It's not my fault!" There is nothing to say to them except, "Stay where you are forever." They just cannot repent and simply say, "I'm sorry."

It could be said that this attitude stems from their "ego," "self-preservation," or "egotism." To express it in a way that is more pleasant to the ear, it is their "pride." It is pride and the attitude to put themselves first.

However, if you really want to put yourself first, you should think about saving yourself. You have to deliver yourself from suffering.

To do so, you must really be sorry if you think you have made a mistake. You cannot imagine how much happiness such a simple truth will bring you. That alone will make you and the other person involved happier, as well as the people around you.

If you make a mistake and hurt another's feelings, apologize

Those with much pride are eager to save themselves first. They will do anything to get an advantage or benefit themselves. In such situations, if they make a mistake they should apologize.

If you feel you have offended someone's feelings, even if it was a misunderstanding, it is certain that you were part of the problem that caused the situation. Then you need to have a big heart, admitting, "It was probably my mistake. The manner of my expression was not quite appropriate."

It is impossible to have perfect communication between people. You may want to say, "I didn't mean that, but people misunderstood me." However, if you did not manage to convey your true intention, this would mean there was a problem in your communication, and you must admit that.

It was because of your poorly expressed feelings and thoughts. You have to admit your shortcoming in the way you communicated. You may want to insist, "That's not what I really meant, and it's not my fault," but if you could not make yourself understood, it is an issue of poor communication. Even if you later say, "The truth was that I really cared," it may be too late.

As you can see, you should take responsibility for the consequences of poor communication. If another person misunderstood you, it is your responsibility for having made a misleading statement and taken action accordingly. You should at least reflect on this point and make efforts to improve such situations.

Of course, some people may not accept your apology. But if you admit your mistakes and say you are sorry, you will at least be able to sleep peacefully. This much is certain.

4

How to Receive the Words of Others

It should be noted, again and again, that the implication of words should be considered carefully. In human minds, a negative personal remark can easily be taken out of proportion. Even if there was no intention to be so negative, a comment can be taken very seriously.

On the other hand, after receiving a compliment, you might react humbly. The following day, you might even think, "That comment was probably making fun of me, after all." You will not be easily pleased by a compliment, but you would tend to believe negative remarks about you.

People with a tendency to easily believe negative remarks while feeling suspicious of good things said of them will never achieve happiness. Please bear this truth in mind. If you happen to have such a character, it would seem that you would be an example of a person with the "unhappiness syndrome" described in Chapter 2 of my book *Unhappiness Syndrome*. I feel people like this can easily be found.

I suspect this to be the case with the majority of women. Perhaps more than half of women do not know how to deal with compliments. On the other hand, if they received bad comments about themselves, they would take them too seriously, even magnifying the negative impact tenfold.

Actually, such a tendency can be overcome with your own efforts. You must do this, otherwise the realm of hell within your mind will grow larger. If you have received even a small compliment, it is very important to simply be happy.

5

Be Thankful for Receiving a Critical Remark

Those who can reply, "Thank you," when scolded are "heroes"

Another matter I would like to discuss is how to react to negative comments. There are several ways to deal with this situation. If you are criticized by someone, you may want to fight back, feeling as if your whole character has been attacked. However, please do not immediately react to the situation. When others say disapproving words to you, the last thing you should do is to react instantly with defiance. This is a reaction of the lowest level. If you were a gorilla or a primitive man, you might feel the need to give blow for blow. But you should know that this kind of behavior is the worst thing for a civilized person.

If you are angrily denounced by someone, pause for five or ten seconds. This is what I suggest first. Hold on for just five or ten seconds, and in that short time, quickly think of possible causes for the negative words. Consider if there were reasons for the critical remarks made by the other person.

Even if you determine that you were not wrong, consider further whether there was room for misunderstanding. For example, was there any possibility of a mistake because of poor communication on your part?

If you think there is the slightest chance of misunderstanding, you should first accept the criticism. Accept the words, thinking, "I didn't make enough effort." If you do so, the other person will likely calm down a little. Then, ask, "What exactly was the problem? Please tell me about it for my future reference."

In this way, when another person makes any angry comments, if you feel such comments make sense, first accept them, saying, "Thank you."

Very few people are able to say "thank you" in the face of critical comments. I would call them "heroes." It is very rare to meet such a great person. When you receive severe criticism, if you have the great capacity to say, "Thank you very much for your honest remarks. Please tell me a little more about what I did wrong," I think this is the first step toward becoming a great personality.

Your honest attitude can change another

You should understand that very few people have this great capacity. Indeed, I myself was often admonished by high spirits in the early days, but it is understood that I have sufficient capacity to bear such remarks. While being criticized often, I continued to work cheerfully. Saying, "I'm sorry. What was the problem?" or "Oh, is that what I did wrong? I understand. I will do better next time," I carried on making efforts.

You may meet people who habitually badmouth others, are always criticizing, and are so harsh that they are avoided by all. Yet this kind of person will not know how to react if you say "thank you" and ask them to correct you. They would be speechless. They would then realize they were behaving childishly.

If you are unyielding to criticism and push back, that would not be productive, but if you act in a more civil way, the other person may begin to change. You need to be aware of this.

This attitude, however, concerns general cases, so you should be flexible and take matters on a case-by-case basis. If you converse with criminals and say things like, "Please teach me a lesson," you would make a fool of yourself. So please act in moderation. That is when you need to be particularly attentive.

6

Cultivating People with Words

Sometimes you have to be deliberately harsh to scold someone

I would like to make another point regarding the use of words. I want to say that there is a difference between scolding and venting your anger. When necessary, you sometimes have to use harsh language. Do not forget this.

When you think another person is making a mistake, you have to tell the person about it. It is just like warning a child of the danger of crossing the street when the traffic light is red. At that point, you have to say firmly and loudly, "Wait! Don't walk!"

Similarly, when a person is about to enter a dangerous situation at the crossroads of their life, let us say, as if they are about to fall off a cliff, that is when you have to save them, even if you have to suddenly punch or push them. This may result in having to say harsh words. There are some situations in life where you need to be blunt.

Many people suffer because they cannot act in a harsh manner when necessary. Such types are very common among people who are religious. With regret, they often have thoughts like, "I couldn't say one word about..." Religious personalities may often suffer in this way, especially concerning relationship issues. If they just spend their time thinking, "This cannot be right," and are unable to say the necessary words, they will gradually drift in an undesirable direction. The lack of courage to say what is necessary can result in having to repent for a mistake, as well as the other person having to feel very sorry, too.

This is a troublesome aspect for the type of people who study Buddha's Truth. It must be difficult to be deliberately harsh, but sometimes it is required. In such a situation, you have to act sternly, imagining yourself as if you were an actor. Sometimes you have to be authoritarian given the time and situation. When you really have to save someone, you might have to be the "bad guy" and behave harshly.

I myself have experienced this kind of situation many times. As you study and practice the Truth, you want to be a good person, so you want to avoid speaking to others in a strict manner. You might wish you did not have to use disciplinary words, and instead say only what is pleasing to the ears of others. However, if you continue that way, other people may gradually become conceited and go astray.

Therefore, when you recognize another person about to do something dangerous, you have to remind them outright. If you fail to say so, they will lose their lives. To allow them to corrupt their minds is the same as letting them lose their lives. So, you must not let them commit evil. In such cases, you must decide to behave in a severe manner to warn them.

Having reached a critical point, give admonitions in a step-by-step manner

If you work in an organization, you will likely encounter similar scenarios. You may find that some of your subordinates and co-workers are acting wrongfully. In the daily routine, you may bear the actions of such people to a certain extent. However, when you reckon they have crossed a certain danger point, you definitely have to caution them.

If you hear someone say, "I am warning you for the first time," "This is my second warning," or "Be careful of my third warning," it would cause you to pause. I actually used to say these words when I worked in a trading company. "First warning," "second warning," and "be prepared for the next" are alerts I used to give. I was strict at the time, and such warnings made my juniors and subordinates be careful. I usually smile now that I am the CEO of Happy Science, but the truth is, I can be very intimidating. I would observe and let them act freely, but sometimes I had to say, "This is my first caution, so remember it," or "This is the second time." Usually, I did not have to give a third warning, as the situation would change for the better after the second warning. Sometimes, warnings are required.

This might even occur when the person is your boss. There may be occasions when speaking out is not so easy but is necessary.

As it is not good to speak in an outburst when enraged, you should portion out your anger in a timely manner. Some people go out of control, totally losing their temper, and vent their rage violently and explosively. But in doing so, they will have gone beyond the point where any good could be obtained. Human relationships will completely break down, and thereafter these people will be seen as having abnormal personalities. People will think them eccentric, and those who suffered their outrage will be too scared to go near them again. I used to hear stories like that, where younger employees were lectured for a full two hours until they passed out. Some bosses could be that demanding. Again, please do not be so extreme.

So, after observing a certain amount of bad behavior, it would be advisable to split your disciplinary scolding over three sessions. After the first and the second scolding, it would be good to get the situation under control so that the third session is not needed.

It is very important to nurture people with words of praise, but occasionally the opposite holds true, as in the Asian proverb that states, "Good medicine tastes bitter." Sometimes bitter pills need to be swallowed.

It does not mean that you hate them, but there are times when you have to say something unpleasant for their own good. At that point, you should speak decisively. You have to show no leniency when the need arises. Otherwise, you may not be able to end bad behavior. Please bear this truth in mind. But this is not something you have to do often.

What has been described so far is the general explanation of Right Speech. However, according to a more detailed Buddhist perspective, Right Speech can be checked using the following guidelines: Truthful words: Have you spoken words that you are not ashamed of, that would not go against your conscience? Abusive words: Have you hurt others with your words? False words: Have you made false claims about your enlightenment? Flattery words: Have you led others astray to make them conceited? Two-faced speech: Did you say one thing to A and a different thing to B to drive a wedge between them? (Refer to *The Laws of the Sun*, Chapter 2, Section 10.)

Chapter 5

Right Action

正

業

Lecture given on January 14, 1989
at Happy Science Training Hall, Tokyo

1

Professional Ethics in Today's World

In today's society, the standard for right work is not clear

The term Right Action essentially means to act in a rightful manner. You should ask yourself, "Have I done the right things today?" Nowadays you could also consider that this means doing "right work."

The theme Right Action presents us with a very difficult issue in our times. It is because of the complexity of today's society and industrial progress that many people now have almost no idea what the standard for right work should be.

In previous times, it seems that there were simpler standards and specific sets of work ethics. However, in current times the definition of what is right work is an extremely difficult question.

We need to know about the meaning of work in today's society

Another theme we really need to consider is why right work is required, and what kind of spiritual implications the issue of right work would have. You need to be aware of this.

If you have a religious nature, you may tend to spend as much time as you can in spiritual contemplation. You would have an affinity for a contemplative life and long to enter into the world of meditation.

So how should we consider this, to find the solution to the conflict between our yearning for a contemplative life and our jobs and workplace? This is a topic we need to examine from various angles. Unless we work hard to find the best way to solve the conflict, we are not qualified to be born today and be religious persons.

In the past, it would have been enough to give teachings on Exploration of the Right Mind in a contemplative life, and I think it used to be much simpler in a sense.

But how should we view today's society? Should we ignore our jobs entirely? Can they be dismissed as vain? Can we deny today's professions and discard them as expressions of vanity, having no spiritual meaning whatsoever? Or should we consider that there may be some other implication here as well, since we as spirits have incarnated to live in the present time? How should we consider the current state of society in light of the laws of spiritual evolution?

I believe this is a challenge that should not be avoided. It seems to me that we have not yet reached a clear conclusion about this issue of how we think about contemporary professions.

In the past, career advancement, titles, and money were often referred to as wrongful goals from a religious perspective. But if such topics were only viewed in that way, it would not leave room for religious logic to be effective in the business world.

The question is whether it is appropriate that we continue to believe that way.

2

The Laws of Prosperity
in the Historical Flow of Christianity

God's desire to align the prosperity of a country with religious truths

Looking at the plan of the heavenly world, it seems that modifications have obviously been made regarding work and religious belief.

For example, what would have been the attitude toward work in the time of Jesus? Reading the Bible, it is obvious that not much priority was placed on work ethics. It is hard to believe that the preaching of Jesus in those days was done with a clear idea of the industrial society that occurred more than 1,700 years later. If a prosperous society existed in his time, we can presume that Jesus would have taught in accordance with the manner of those times. However, in the social environment of Jesus' time, he would not have had any thought of teaching laws with such advanced prosperity in mind.

It seems that during the period of the Reformation, particularly from the influence of Martin Luther and John Calvin, the issue of religious truth and how it affected the actual lives of people challenged existing institutions and brought about change. The influence of Protestantism on the spirit of capitalism has been significant.

With the Puritans sailing on the Mayflower from England to the New World, a miraculous development occurred in what would become America. Here, I can see God's desire to align the prosperity of a country with religious truths.

A religious way of thinking is also required in business communities

Observing the stream of Christianity throughout the nineteenth and twentieth centuries, we see the rise and development of a belief system that embraced a scientific explanation of the laws of prosperity. It was the so-called New Thought movement in Christianity, and it became very powerful.

Additionally, with regard to Norman Vincent Peale or Robert Schuller, the teachings they preached were initially seen as heretical by the traditional Christian church.

Many of you may have read the book *The Power of Positive Thinking* by Norman Vincent Peale. It has sold more than 20 million copies worldwide, but when it was first published, it was met with severe opposition. He was besieged by objection all around, and the voices of criticism from many church leaders did not cease their loud disapproval. They thought a modern version of Christ's teachings that was business-friendly and useful for the workplace was a distortion of authentic Christian teachings.

Throughout all the negativity however, the book was popular and steadily spread throughout the world. Given the background of this popularity, there was certainly a necessity. Unless a religious way of thinking was adopted for the business community, Christianity could not meet people's demands or needs. Just reading from the Bible as was done in the past was not enough. After all, this religious update was also made based on a plan from the heavenly realm.

3

Prosperity and Development in Buddha's Truth

It is time to address the issues of work and the Truth

Japan is now catching up with the United States, but it used to be said that if you copied what was popular in the United States at a given time, it would be successful in Japan ten years later. The situation has changed since then, but considering the future environment of the business and religious communities in Japan, we need to have a fusional idea that links the two fields. Such an idea should naturally come forth.

Therefore, at Happy Science, we clearly present the concept of progress as part of the Principles of Happiness. Without it, we would not be able to meet the demands of society in the future.

Shakyamuni Buddha's teachings did not include the concept of progress but rather focused on the development of one's internal world. However, today we are immersed in an environment that involves much dynamism, and the development of the internal world alone would not be enough.

I often talk about a "happiness that continues from this world to the other world." As this phrase indicates a connection, the time has come for the realm that once existed only in the Real World to manifest in the world on earth, too.

I feel that the gods of Japanese Shintoism have made a lot of effort in this regard. Considering the reconstruction of postwar Japan, it seems to me that the power of the high-ranking Shinto gods contributed significantly.

In addition to this, I believe it is time to address the issue of work life and the Truth based on a more essential and fundamental point of view.

Not only meditative life, but the principles of development and prosperity are also part of the Truth

I have talked about Hermes of ancient Greece, who was born 4,300 years ago. If you examine the life of Hermes, you will find that Truth was taught in a unique way. The Truth in Hermes' time was different from the meditative life that you all have been thinking of as truth. That Truth clearly contained what was to become the principles of development and prosperity in this world on earth.

In fact, more than 4,000 years ago, Hermes had already anticipated what would later happen in the modern and contemporary periods during the seventeenth, eighteenth, nineteenth, and twentieth centuries. Such principles were already taught then.

It was Hermes who first developed a money-based economy. He also initiated something similar to the present-day foreign exchange system. He already had in place a structure of tripartite trade and an economic union that was similar to the EU of today. With such ideas, Hermes made efforts to create peace based on economic relationships instead of dominating Greece and the Mediterranean world militarily.

In addition, Hermes fostered a concept that would become a precursor of the United Nations. These original ideas already existed more than 4,000 years ago.

After learning this, you will know that the basis of Truth is embedded with a very solid central axis. And I think you will probably come to feel that you cannot ignore the reality of this world on earth or the world of business.

This is because there will be situations in the world where we can realize innovation in a greater manner by shifting the laws that govern society toward the Truth. In that sense, just to avoid the reality of this world would not be enough.

4

Shakyamuni Buddha's Self-Reflection, Hermes' Prosperity – Using the Two Wheels

As I have been teaching from the very beginning, I would like you to understand first of all that we are proceeding using two wheels: Buddha's reflective and contemplative life and Hermes' laws of prosperity and development. Rather than concentrating on just one aspect, I aim to firmly establish both aspects and integrate them.

Please do not forget about these basics. In order to change the times we live in today, one aspect alone will not be enough. Both the "Laws of Buddha" and the "Laws of Hermes" are essential, and furthermore, we need to integrate them both. Based on the integration of the two, a higher concept, or a concept of greater meaning, will emerge.

The time will come when even the "Laws of Buddha" and the "Laws of Hermes" will eventually fade away.

It will not be too far off. In the first and second years of Happy Science, I am already making an evaluation of Buddha's eighty years of life in terms of, for example, the practice of self-reflection. Hermes' life is now being assessed as well [at the time this lecture was originally delivered in 1989]. What exactly will come after this? I would like you to think about this question.

We have learned from and begun to integrate the legacy of the past, and are now even trying to move beyond it.

That means we can see the future and the direction we are headed for. What we will see is the future of humanity, the future society. It is Happy Science that indicates the shape of the future society of humanity.

5

The Japanese Dream Begins from the Realm of Truth

I would also like to predict that this movement of Truth in Japan, starting with Happy Science, will realize the Japanese Dream in a fresh sense.

The American Dream started in the United States. In the twentieth century, the period of the American Dream, people from all walks of life have pursued their dreams and aspirations on the stage of the United States of America.

This notion may have reached its peak. What comes next? It would be a world built on the Japanese Dream.

The Japanese Dream begins from the realm of Truth. With the realm of Truth as the starting point, the Japanese Dream will eventually permeate the world.

What once seemed to originate as economic growth will change color, affecting the entire world as the movement of spreading the Truth flows from Japan.

You are now at the headstream of the movement. The current may still be small.* But in time, I think you will realize that this

---

* As of the year 2021, thirty-two years after this lecture, Happy Science is working to create the future civilization through its many activities in fields such as politics, education, movies, and music.

small stream will broaden into a great river that flows into the future society. The people of the world do not yet understand the magnitude of this movement, which I described in my book *The Laws of the Sun*, but the time will come when it becomes clear in people's minds.

We are able to view today's society and the future society in relation to Right Action. It is a good occasion to evaluate "what the purpose of work is" from a fresh perspective.

6

Right Action Contributes to the Evolution of the Soul

Developing leadership skills through work

If asked, "Does training, discipline, and effort in one's work have any effect on the soul?" I would have to say that it does, to a great extent. That is my conclusion.

In my observance of higher level spirits in the Spirit World, the more evolved spirits are, the more extensive their activities regarding the actual work they do. In fact, high spirits carry out a broad range of work.

This is because as a soul evolves through spiritual training, the challenge to improve leadership is still applicable, even in the ninth dimension. The mission to be better leaders remains a goal of soul training even in the higher spiritual realms. From the sixth dimension and higher, spirits study the process of the evolution of becoming leaders, and their soul training in terms of leadership continues.

In order to increase your leadership ability, you have to be able to perform the work that you oversee.

Even high spirits in heaven must be born on earth from time to time to acquire earthly experience in order to develop leadership skills. Otherwise, their leadership skills will gradually diminish.

If they remain in the higher spiritual realms for a long time, their understanding of the earthly environment and society begins to fade. The gap between their sense of the Spirit World and their sense of the earthly world gradually widens. Then, as many spirits who have experienced earthly lives return to the Real World, the high spirits have difficulties in guiding them.

As you can see, even the spirits from higher dimensions are incarnated not only for salvation but also to improve their work abilities. By developing their work skills, they can perform even greater work when they return to the Real World. Work in the earthly world is indeed a very valuable experience for the soul.

Work of salvation can be measured in terms of work capacity

I mentioned in my book *The Laws of the Sun* that Right Action can be associated with "nurturing love," the love of the sixth dimension. However, Right Action involves elements that are also manifested in the highest realms. There is no doubt that God or Buddha has outstanding abilities to carry out work, and He has accomplished so much.

I am now working on a mission of integrating the laws of the ninth dimension; El Cantare is providing guidance in His capacity as the consciousness to integrate the ninth-dimensional laws. It is work to unify the opinions of the ten spirits in the ninth dimension.

He is the very existence that people on earth have been revering as the "Heavenly Father." There exists such a great consciousness.

Our salvation work at Happy Science, if observed within a larger framework, can also be measured in one aspect by how well the work is being done.

7

Work Is the Basis of Building a Utopia

Strive to do the best you can in the environment you inhabit

I have been pointing out for some time that if you work in an office or some other business but cannot build a utopia or cannot perform your required job, you cannot make yourself useful at Happy Science. Happy Science is not some fairyland.

After all, people who are able to offer useful skills elsewhere can accomplish more in the activities of Happy Science. I hope you do not misunderstand this.

If you think, "I've never been successful anywhere in this world, couldn't find contentment, and never managed to build a utopia, but I'll surely achieve all those at Happy Science," that will not be good enough.

As I said in my book *The Laws of Success*, there is much preparation to do in order to enter the City of the Successful.

Therefore, even if you see the worthiness of the movement of spreading the Truth, you cannot be satisfied with just being part of it. This means that you need to build up your strength through basic training in other fields.

The same can be said for women in this regard. I believe many women are employed in jobs, but for those who are homemakers and are taking care of your families, you must remember the perspective that the job of homemaking is also a discipline of Right Action.

At the very least, the starting point for creating a utopia is the desire to help others. If you cannot take the first step toward building a utopia at home, it is hard to imagine you can take the larger leap of helping to create an ideal world.

So I would like you to take a look at where you stand. Take another look at your current situation as a housewife, a business person, or an office worker.

There are certainly environmental factors, and these environmental factors may at times prevent you from achieving your full potential. However, it is only when you do your best where you are situated that you can achieve more in other places. This is the truth. If you abandon any efforts to learn in your current position or circumstances and expect to do better in realizing your full potential somewhere else, this is very naive. Such fragile illusions will only vanish in the end. I would like you to think about this deeply.

No job you are given in this world is in vain

I myself had to fulfill various responsibilities before starting this movement of Truth. Even after my Great Enlightenment, I spent a lot of time preparing to establish Happy Science. When I actually began my activities, I had a keen realization: "None of what I have done so far was in vain."

If I had cut corners in the earlier stages of my life, this could have easily had a significant negative impact on my current work.

This feeling gets deeper and deeper, year by year, month by month, day by day. Rather, I regret that I did not experience even more intense soul training. I feel strongly that "there was still much to learn as a human being before pursuing the world of spirits or divinity and the like. I may not have learned enough." I have a very strong feeling that if I could get in a time machine to go back in time, I would have learned and accomplished things more thoroughly.

In that sense, nothing is in vain. If you feel you have wasted your energy and time, it is probably because you have not made the most of your experience. It is because you have no intention of making the most of it. No job you are given in this world is a waste. All the experiences from work will not only be nourishment for the soul, but also positive tools for building a utopia. We must know this deeply.

8

Work and Labor

Write down a list of your work roles on a piece of paper

Before you start self-reflection on Right Action, you must first consider the content of your work at present. You need to think about what work is.

What kinds of work have you been given? You can consider any work as a synonym for a role to fulfill. When you think about what your different jobs or roles are, you can probably write a list of them on a piece of paper. Some of you may have more work roles than you can easily count, but most of you can probably list your roles on a single sheet of paper. With some of the roles, you have to consider what and how you are fulfilling them in relation to others.

For example, you may be the president of a company, and your roles fall into several categories. There must be some other roles you are fulfilling besides being a business leader. At home, you may be a father. Fulfilling the responsibilities of fatherhood is also a job. In addition, you will have relations in many other fields, and you will have a role to play in them as well. We are all participating in some kind of community in one way or another.

For each role, consider whether it is "work" or "labor"

I would like you to single out each of the roles and think, "Am I sufficiently fulfilling this role?"

Taking this point further, you could divide each role into two parts, which would identify activities as either "work" to achieve a higher level or "labor" to get something done.

The concept of labor concerns certain repetitive tasks involving processes you are required to do. They are indispensable actions for all to live as human beings. What you have to do every day to survive can be called labor.

If we think about work as a higher-ranking concept than labor, it would include the idea of productivity. It is about how much extra value you are able to create through your actions.

If you think this way, you would see these two parts in every role. For a homemaker, the tasks of making breakfast, lunch, and dinner can be broadly divided into two categories: Those that are necessary can be thought of as labor, and those that are intentional can be thought of as work. This is my perception of the difference between work and labor.

9

Motherhood as a Job

How to incorporate mental value to differentiate "work" from "labor"

With cooking, for example, you could do it with "full dedication." If you cook with the clear intention of caring for the health of your children and husband, giving consideration to balanced nutrition for them with their physical conditions and activities in mind, that would make your cooking effort "work." However, if you are just putting together randomly available ingredients without any particular plan, it would be called "labor."

Depending on how much mental value is committed, the result can be divided into two categories, although outwardly they may appear similar.

Also, if you are a mother, educating your children can be called your vocation. If you believe you are fulfilling your role as a mother by merely scolding or telling your children what to do, actions that serve as outlets for your own frustrations, complaints, and grumblings, then this role is not considered productive. Therefore, it would just be considered "labor" rather than "work."

As a mother, you would naturally try to control your children's bad behavior, but if it does not produce anything good, then this job would be "labor." On the other hand, if the scolding is done so that the children will grow into adults who can contribute to society in the future, then it can be called "work."

Nowadays, many social issues can be traced back to the home life; being a mother is underestimated. Some young office workers are able to do a good job while others cannot, and the root of the problem is often found in their earlier home lives. Those who did not receive an adequate basic education at home will bring this insufficiency into their workplaces, leading to all sorts of problems.

What would happen if the training that should have been done at home were to occur in the workplace? That person would start work with a handicap. This is how many problems start to surface.

One of the basic purposes of raising children is to provide them with the ability to enter the workforce without any shortcomings. They should be taught about the basics of human relationships and how to live as good human beings.

If they did not receive such a fundamental education at home, they will have to experience a great deal more trial and error in their working life. There will be more scolding for them from their bosses, or they will cause disharmony at work. This is because an important part of the home education was not completed. If you could seek the origin of these problems, it might be that the mother was not doing a suitable job.

Creating an excellent environment at home through ingenuity

Nowadays, most workplaces conduct performance reviews. Employees are rated, and these ratings are the basis for salaries and bonuses.

What if a rating system were applied to homemaking or motherhood? There should certainly be a difference in the abilities of mothers. It would be wrong to think ratings were only for workplaces and could not be applied to homemaking or motherhood. There definitely are differences.

Motherhood can be measured according to the abilities of mothers. There could be ratings such as above-average, exceptional, or below-average. Furthermore, what happens to children who are raised by a mother who is rated "below-average"? They are already behind at their starting points in work life. In the long run, a lower evaluation for these children at work will be reflected in their future levels of happiness.

Besides motherhood, a housewife would also be evaluated based on her skills in home management. A homemaker would never be valued less than a supermarket cashier, for example. Rather, homemaking is one of the most valuable jobs; it is of great importance to create a nurturing environment at home using ingenuity.

You may think that making money is what matters. However, although you make money in a certain job, it may merely be labor. Even if a job is not highly paid, it might be productive work. Homemaking can become "work" as opposed to "labor." So, abandoning this responsibility would not lead to realizing one's full potential in the realm of Truth.

Making efforts to put your soul into your job

As you might understand, issues concerning work are quite wide-ranging. There exists a vast spectrum of jobs, and the work behaviors required for each job are also extremely diverse.

However, what I can say is that in order for you to at least "practice Right Action," you have to exert your full potential in your activities at work.

For you to exert your full potential, you need to find meaning in your life on earth in the work you do. You need to be able to express the meaning of your arrival into this world.

You should make efforts to put your soul into your work. If you instead end up spending time aimlessly at work, it would be a great shame. It is very disappointing to live with such an attitude, and it will be discussed further in relation to Right Living, which comes next in the Eightfold Path. One of the most important elements in the practice of Right Action is to be able to exert your full potential.

10

Invincible Thinking in the Workplace

Learn lessons from disappointment and make more efforts when successful

Another important thing is that you must not forget the attitude of continuous learning in the workplace.

At work, there will be plenty of things that do not go the way you want them to. You may be reluctant to accept this fact. There will be times when you think you are doing the best job you can, but you do not get the recognition you think you deserve, or something will get in your way.

However, I think this is a good opportunity to reconsider your situation. Whenever you experience setbacks, obstructions, or disappointments, you must always ask yourself, "What can I learn from this?" There is always something to learn. This viewpoint should not be overlooked.

If you are able to have the mindset that "nothing in this world is in vain," even when things do not work out, you can think that "there must be some lesson to be learned." If you can look at things from this perspective, you may find that they can make sense. And the lesson you learn will surely be used for the next opportunity. Do not forget this.

Yet another element to be aware of regarding Right Action is the attitude to have when you are becoming successful or making progress at work.

I have previously said many times that it is more difficult to deal with times of success rather than times of disappointment or frustration. I have reiterated this again and again. This is because it is human nature to be satisfied with oneself and one's small successes and thus to become complacent.

Therefore, it is important to reaffirm your position when you think you are moving upward. Also, the more people praise you, the humbler you should become. As soon as you think you have achieved success, it will be the start of the next stage. You should never forget that this is the very moment for you to begin making further efforts with a fresh start.

This way of thinking is what I call "invincible thinking," which includes the following ideas: "In times of disappointment and frustration, you always learn a lesson"; and oppositely, "When you are successful, you should work even harder." With these attitudes, you will never fail in life.

If you think, "I have been so successful with God's blessing and the power of my guardian and guiding spirits," then you should think, "I'm going to try even harder to live up to their expectations." Conversely, as soon as you start thinking, "I've achieved success on my own, without help from anyone else," and continue with that belief, your spiritual growth will halt there.

The more opportunities you are given, the more you must attempt to take the next step

The more opportunities you are offered, the harder you should work to attain the next step. This is exactly when you need to keep motivated and continue to make efforts; otherwise, you will only achieve limited success and mediocre results. You always have to take the next step. When you find yourself in a favorable situation, think, "Okay, I have to give something in return for this. As a response to this benefit, I'll take another step to achieve something greater. I'll do something more to help people." On the contrary, if you become self-satisfied, it will end your progress.

When you look back on the past year, you will probably find some events that were unfortunate and make you unhappy and frustrated at work. What did you think on those occasions? Did you learn any lesson to prepare for the next challenge?

On the other hand, what did you do when you were successful? When successful, did you think, "I must not be satisfied with this. It was not an achievement I did on my own. With the light of many to show me the way and the power of many supporting me, I stand here today. So, I need to return this goodwill provided by them." Or did you take for granted that you completely deserved the position you were given?

11

Attitude of Being Thankful for Your Circumstances

*Do not make the mistake of attributing
your success to your own effort,
but rather be grateful to those around you*

Sometimes we have false ideas: Even though we do not shine on our own, but only reflect the light of others like the moon reflects sunlight, we often mistakenly think of ourselves as the "sun."

This can be said of all of you, each and every one of you. Although you may shine like the moon by reflecting light, there are times when you think you shine like the sun, on your own doing. This is a very dangerous moment.

I think people who work in large corporations are especially at risk for this kind of danger. It is easy to think, "This is all because of my ability." When projects move forward and business dealings go smoothly, it is easy to attribute the success to your own ability and competence, but it is often the company name that is doing the job. This is also the case for those who work in government offices. You can only do your job sufficiently because you have the backing of your organization. If you think about what happens when this backing is taken away, you will find yourself quite helpless.

You will realize it was not a job that you could have done on your own personal merit. The organization's name recognition and network may have been the driving force of your situation. If you mistakenly think that the success was attributable to your personal talent or ability, you will then start to experience suffering.

There are many cases of high-ranking civil servants getting top jobs in private sector companies after they retire from government work. With this "privileged pass," former civil service administrators may succeed in their second careers. These people may have abilities relevant to their new positions, but the opposite is very common.

I have seen quite a few bad cases. People who rise above a certain level of governmental work and then change jobs using their "privileged passes" are not always so successful. There are plenty of people in such situations who just take advantage of the positions to get good salaries. In truth, these people are just being used by the organization as handy fill-ins. They mistake the power of the organization for their own abilities. The truth is that they are not really capable; it is the former government position that is doing the job, not the person, so to speak.

The same can be said of some managers or executives of private sector companies. They may think, "This company couldn't survive without me," but the company would most likely continue after they have left. Even if they were to think, "Without me, this division will never run smoothly," their replacement would quickly manage to do so. After all, such thinking is often based on much misunderstanding.

In many cases, about 80% of success is because of the power of the organizations, the power of the corporations, or the collective power of the members of the organization. Only the remaining 20% is variable, the part that is colored by individual personalities as if adding spices to a dish of food. There is often confusion about these factors, so you have to think carefully. Even if you are currently successful, it is important not to attribute the success only to your own abilities and efforts. Instead, carefully analyze the factors that contributed to the achievement, and be grateful for the people who have supported you.

As I have mentioned in my book *The Laws of Success*, no one can achieve success without the favor of others. You can think that the possibility of individual success is virtually zero, because human society is structured that way.

There may be a world like Robinson Crusoe's, where he lives and works by himself, but even in his case, his life got better after he encountered Friday, his servant. Progress does not come easily on its own.

Do not criticize your boss or those who are in positions to promote you

Another common misunderstanding is often seen among those with religious natures. Those who have a tendency to "oppose the powerful" may be found among you.

Some people who study religious truth tend to dismiss worldly power or those who are successful. Furthermore, they are likely to think, "I don't belong to their world, but somewhere else." At that point, they may start to criticize their boss or someone in a position to promote them. I have to say that they do not know the principles of success.

If you always side with lower-ranking workers against authority, you will never get ahead. That is because of certain dynamics. The type of person who becomes most successful is the one who is supported by superiors and loved by subordinates.

When you change jobs, you will realize how well-liked you were by the people you worked with. It would be very sad to find that no one is bothered at all, or that no one said that they would miss you. Sometimes you may find yourself in such a situation.

So we must carefully note our circumstances when we think we are successful. We should ask ourselves questions like, "Isn't my current achievement due to the help of others? Am I grateful to them? Have I paid back their favor? Does this feeling of gratitude produce a new step toward further self-improvement and self-help efforts?" Always remember the allegory of the sun and the moon.

What is written above is a modern way of explaining Right Action.

In the fundamental Buddhism taught by Shakyamuni Buddha, Right Action can be thought of as "right conduct," which is the root of "karma" that is carried with one at the time of reincarnation. In other words, the self-reflection of Right Action focuses on actions that have violated religious precepts, laws, societal morals, or criminal acts. (Refer to *The Laws of the Sun*, Chapter 2, Section 10.)

Chapter 6

Right Living

正
命

Lecture given on January 14, 1989
at Happy Science Training Hall, Tokyo

1

The Modern Meaning of Right Living

Right Living is about making
the most effective use of your time and lifestyle

I would like to talk about the topic of living rightly. The difference between Right Action and Right Living can be explained as the difference between how you work and how you spend your daily life, but Right Living has more implications. To put it in modern terms, we can think of Right Living as the question of how to make the best use of your time. There are many books on the market about how to make the most of your time, and I am sure many of you have read them.

Right Living may also be expressed with another word, "lifestyle." Here you are asked, "What kind of lifestyle are you willing to choose?" "How do you like to spend your time?" "What kind of lifestyle do you choose?" These questions are still relevant today.

As an office worker in today's society, suppose you are asked, "What is your ideal lifestyle?" You would then understand the difference between Right Action and Right Living. It is related to the way you spend your time after work. With the perspective of Right Living, you are asked how you live after the work day. How have you spent most of your time outside the restrictions of working hours? What are the results of such activities? What will happen in the future? I would like you to ask yourself these questions.

All human beings are equally subject to time, but differentiate themselves depending on how they spend their time

I know someone who compared time to gold coins. The parable goes, "Every morning, people wake up with twenty-four gold coins in their pockets. As one looks around, many people will be seen walking about and taking the coins from their pockets to toss them into a ditch. They don't realize how ridiculous their behavior is. The truth is that time is worth more than gold coins. Of course, there are various people who think it's mad to throw away gold coins, but they don't care at all about throwing away time. It's really sad."

That was the allegorical story that was told.

Also, as I wrote in my book *The Golden Laws*, it is quite important to consider the equality shared by all in the time frame of a twenty-four-hour day.

Thinking of the aspects under which each person could be seen as equal, there is nothing more obvious than the equality of time. No matter what kind of person you are, you are only given twenty-four hours a day. One person can use the twenty-four hours to become a great figure, while another may end up doing harm to society.

It is known that heaven and hell exist in the afterlife, and that they are separate destinations that are the consequences of how you spend time while alive. The question to be considered is for what purpose you spend your personal time.

2

Increase the Value of Truth per Unit of Time

Reflect on how you use your time daily
from the viewpoint of contributing to building a utopia

Time management is an essential factor in considering the Truth of Buddha in modern life, and this consideration cannot be avoided. Moreover, we need to consider the management of not only "relative time," which can be measured by a clock, but also "absolute time." It is about improving the efficiency of each hour you spend.

The time efficiency I am talking about here is more than just work efficiency, such as the efficiency of time spent for carrying goods. Rather, it is about increasing utopian value or the value of Truth attained in an hour. If you calculate a person's "contribution to utopia" or "contribution to the Truth" using a twenty-four-hour period as a time unit, a sort of average can be obtained. It is absolutely necessary to increase this average, and it is the secret of turning your life into gold.

This perspective is very important in self-reflection. Reflecting on "how one lived and spent one's day" can be somewhat vague and hard to practice, but if you reflect on the idea in terms of time, you will be able to understand more clearly. I recommend that you practice self-reflection in terms of time, as in "how did you spend your time?"

Reflect on how you have used your time from when you wake up in the morning until you go to bed at night. Then measure how you have improved in efficiency in how you spend your time. Here I am not only referring to work efficiency. You should reflect on how time-efficient you have become from the perspective of the Truth or building utopia, or if you have spent much time doing activities unrelated to those values.

The value of Truth in doing a job adequately without mistakes

In desk work, doing a job proficiently has its own value of Truth. The work may only affect a limited group of people, but the work can still be useful to others.

As you can see, I am not just talking about the movement of spreading the Truth. If you are doing a good job, a proper job working as a regular office worker, it can be said you are producing positive values of Truth. On the other hand, if you make mistakes at work, or cause trouble for your colleagues or clients, then those disturbing factors will be considered negative in terms of the value of Truth.

Therefore, it is important to look at what you have achieved at work per unit of time. This is a typical method of self-reflection from the perspective of Right Living.

There are similarities between Right Action and Right Living. Right Living can be considered in terms of how one spends time during a day. On the other hand, Right Action can be considered in terms of one's work style in a broader sense, how one should live, or in terms of the value determined by one's actions.

3

A Lifestyle of Investing in the Future

Use your free time to invest in your future

Another theme to discuss is the style of living itself.

What do you think your ideal lifestyle should be at present? I would like you to ask yourself this question. I would then like you to enlarge your time frame from the present to a medium-term and long-term perspective, and ask yourself, "What would be my ideal? What kind of life will I be satisfied with?" Deciding how to live your life with a scope of five years, ten years, or even longer can be included in Right Living.

A particularly important point in discussing lifestyle is how you use your free time. This means thinking about how you spend time aside from work or doing necessary tasks.

The twenty-four-hour day includes the time used for basic living chores as well as your job. After taking out those hours, use the remaining time available to design what your future should be. This would be your life project. It is drawing up a plan for your life and putting it into practice. I believe that you should at least have some ideals when considering your lifestyle. You should not go about your life living aimlessly.

Build up your lifestyle, your pattern of life, and make sure to include time to plan to invest in your future. I think it is important to include activities that will be beneficial for you later on. Build assets in your life plan that will help you live as a useful person, as an excellent person, as one who is helpful, and who will be appreciated by others no matter what kind of environment or what kind of relationships you will be involved in. I think this is important.

You might like to read, listen to music, do exercises, or take cultural courses. There are many ways to spend your time, but you need to think about your activities from the perspective of investing in the future.

Find a way of living that will help set firm roots and develop a stronger tree trunk

Taking myself for example, some of the books I have been reading lately will not be useful to me immediately, but they should be relevant in a few more years. So I am building up my stock of information for the next few years. In this way, I am always preparing for the future at any given time.

In this book, I am teaching about the method of self-reflection, which is not necessarily connected to what I am reading at present. This is not the only matter I am thinking about; I am working on many other themes as well. I envisage the future three, five, ten, twenty, and even thirty years from now and am accumulating material for those times. In this way, I am setting down my roots firmly, so to speak, exploring many things. It can be said that because of such a firm footing, I am capable of weathering difficult times. I covered this subject in my book *An Unshakable Mind*.

In Right Living, the idea of setting down firm roots is important. In the practice of Right Action concerning work, you may focus on doing the best you can do in the place you are assigned. On the other hand, Right Living involves the practice of developing a stronger tree trunk of your life and firmly putting down roots. This practice will allow you leeway and provide resources to help you learn and understand the ideas of different people while having a broad range of perspectives.

Therefore, I would like you to think of the idea of building up a margin when you practice Right Living, if possible. I urge you to develop an investment strategy that will allow you to cultivate your minds and build up physical strength, so that even if you leave your current position, you will still have a store of resources as a good person in order to help others in a variety of ways. This is a modern way of living.

Those who fail to consider this perspective will soon end up becoming like the grasshopper in the fable "The Ant and the Grasshopper." I am sure you all know this story:

During the summer months, the ant works feverishly to stock up on food, but the grasshopper spends his whole time singing, taking the abundance of food for granted. However, when winter comes, there is no more food, so the grasshopper begs the ant to share his food. But the ant says, "What were you doing all summer?" That is how the story goes, and this situation can actually happen in the human world.

Seek a way of living in which you set down firm roots and develop a stronger tree trunk. Right Living is proactive self-reflection that helps you to live a positive life. I would recommend that you practice this kind of proactive self-reflection.

The above is an explanation of Right Living from a modern perspective. In traditional Buddhist terms, Right Living means to live while harmonizing one's action, speech, and thoughts; you are expected to reflect on whether you committed any sin with your body, if the words that came out of your mouth were appropriate, and if there was no wickedness in your thoughts throughout the day. It means reflecting on having a total balance. It is also important to reflect on whether you distanced yourself from drinking, smoking, gambling, drug abuse, and inappropriate sexual behavior. (Refer to *The Laws of the Sun*, Chapter 2, Section 10.)

Chapter 7

Right Effort

正
精
進

Lecture given on January 21, 1989
at Happy Science Training Hall, Tokyo

1

Making Efforts to Follow
the Mind of God or Buddha

Maintaining enlightenment is most difficult

Right Effort means to make efforts on the right path. Buddhism places great emphasis on striving to keep on the path of Truth.

In Chapter 3 of this book, on Right Thought, I talked about the self-help attitude. You may find some overlap, but the self-help effort in connection to Right Thought deals with general aspects, whereas the practice of Right Effort is more specific and individualized. The question is, "What are the essential attitudes of those who are truly seeking enlightenment?"

I would like you to consider Right Effort as one's effort to focus on the path toward enlightenment. It is not the same as making efforts in business dealings. It is about maintaining progress in the direction of God or Buddha. If you were to practice Right Effort in your job, it would be important to make sure to orient your energy toward the construction of utopia and the realization of the will of God or Buddha. This would be a prerequisite for Right Effort.

Now, I would say there are several criteria in making efforts on the right path.

How would you all judge whether or not you are making efforts on the right path? How would you make decisions? At this point, I ask you to reexamine what spiritual discipline means.

In the last chapter of my book *The Essence of Buddha*, I wrote about "The Philosophy of Human Perfection." In it, my intention was to write about how difficult the path to enlightenment can be.

The possibility is open to all. It is also possible to reach a certain level momentarily, but what is difficult to maintain is enlightenment.

You need to gain the insight that the essential point of enlightenment is its maintenance. Needless to say, the process of attaining enlightenment is difficult, but you have to know that the most difficult part is to maintain enlightenment.

You should understand that no matter how many people become enlightened temporarily, like for a day or two, it would not cause the world to suddenly get better. Only when one's enlightenment has been kept up for ten or twenty years does it become an integral part of you.

Therefore, I would like you to understand that no easy way is allowed in attaining enlightenment.

The study of Buddha's Truth and its results are an "entry ticket" to enlightenment, not a "ticket to ride"

I would like to say to those of you who have passed the advanced exam [at our qualification seminar] and received a certificate:

You have been certified to have achieved a certain degree of understanding of Buddha's Truth and have shown that your state of mind has reached a certain level. However, this means that you are standing at the gateway of enlightenment, not that you have become enlightened.

If you get this wrong, you can easily fall down in an instant, or within a day. Please do not be mistaken about this.

Getting a certificate is not a guarantee that you will be reborn as an angel in heaven. It means that you are just standing at the doorstep of enlightenment, nothing more than that.

The study of Buddha's Truth and its results are an "entry ticket" to enlightenment, not a "ticket to ride."

You cannot easily claim that you are enlightened. Only when you have built confidence and maintained an unwavering state of mind for ten years, twenty years, or even longer, until the end of your life on earth, after you have achieved an awareness that you can endure in any kind of environment and you have achieved tangible results, then you can say that you are "enlightened." This is not the same as standing on the threshold of enlightenment.

You can never become accomplished in a year or two. It has only been a little over two years since the establishment of Happy Science [at the time of the lecture]. You can assume that no one would have become enlightened in such a short while. Some of you may have stood at the gateway of enlightenment, and others are walking the path toward it. However, no one is enlightened yet.

It does not matter that you scored highly on the exam, it just means that you are standing at the entrance. It is an admission ticket to the path, but you need to make a continuous effort to use it as a ticket to ride.

Even if you reach a certain state of mind, if you become uncertain and waver when the environment around you changes, that would show your limitation. You may be able to study in a good state of mind because you are presently comfortable and free of worries, but while maintaining that state, a completely different environment may emerge. If you cannot get through adverse conditions, that enlightenment can be easily disrupted.

2

The Difficulty of Maintaining Enlightenment

Younger people may be easily disrupted in maintaining their enlightenment

I would like to point out that it is especially important for young people to maintain enlightenment.

Age has nothing to do with enlightenment. As I have observed the spiritual destination of people who died in their twenties, thirties, forties, fifties, or sixties, I can say that their state of mind had nothing to do with their age.

Some people attain a high state of mind at a young age, while others reach a high state after middle age. Actually, in many cases, people's minds tend to become clouded after middle age, causing them spiritual decline. In this sense, it can be said that age is irrelevant to attaining enlightenment.

However, I have to say that age can be a concern to the maintenance of enlightenment.

Young people can indeed stand at the gateway of enlightenment sooner because they have not yet tainted their minds. Because they have not experienced so many challenges, their minds are less cloudy, and it is easier for them to stand at the gateway of enlightenment.

They have not yet met with life's challenges and not suffered much detriment. Having been brought up in a sheltered environment, they may easily give in when encountering difficult situations. They are fragile in maintaining enlightenment, so to speak. I would like you to understand that younger people may have these weak points.

Consider, for example, that if some people achieve enlightenment measured at 100 points in their twenties, the 100 points will very likely diminish as they age into their thirties, forties, and fifties. There is a very strong possibility that every time they encounter a bad situation, five points, ten points, or fifteen points will be deducted.

On the other hand, consider those in their forties or fifties who attain an enlightenment that is valued at 80 points; as they have come through so many rough patches, the 80 will not diminish so easily, even if two or three points may be lost due to minor incidents.

Instead, it is hard for them to build up an enlightenment that reaches 100, and it may be hard to add one or two points because they are not so pure anymore. However, what they have built up would not easily decline.

As you can see, both age groups have advantages and disadvantages.

Increase your light over the passage of time and flow of experience

There are different levels of enlightenment, but for your own enlightenment to become genuine, you have to undergo the tests called "experience." You must build toughness just as steel is tempered by fire and water.

It is only when you have gone through various experiences and survived challenges to finally reach the end of your life that you can say you have attained enlightenment.

Assuming you have managed to reach a certain level of enlightenment, what would happen if you were faced with financial collapse? What would happen if one of your immediate family members died? What would happen if you were demoted from an executive job position? What would happen if you were about to divorce?

There will be many difficult situations in your life, but please consider them as times when you are being tested. Those who can maintain their steadfastness and continue making efforts during difficult times can be called authentic. On the other hand, for those who collapse easily, their enlightenment should be considered nothing but a mirage.

Therefore, I would like to emphasize the importance of increasing one's light over the passage of time in the flow of one's life experiences.

From year to year your state of mind may alter, and each year you may continue to study Buddha's Truth. Nevertheless, you should have a willingness to put your studies into practice in actual life and test the firmness of your enlightenment.

If you feel enlightened as a student, when you find a job you may not know how it will affect you. What happens when you get promoted and have more responsibility? If you become a manager, will that enlightenment still be meaningful?

If you are a young woman, what would happen if you got married? Could you maintain that enlightenment, or would it completely change? If you are a married woman, what would happen if your husband's position, occupation, income, or any other condition changed?

You would be challenged by such questions.

3

Demonstrate Your Knowledge through Practice

I would like to stress that "No matter how much Truth you have learned, if you are perceived as an eccentric or strange person in actual life, you will not be accepted."

Our goal is to nurture people who would serve as human resources that would be appreciated anywhere. People who only find acceptance in groups that study the Truth, but not in the secular society, will never change the world, no matter how many such people are turned out. When you are successful in bettering your mind through the study of Buddha's Truth, and if you are capable of giving the light of the Truth back to the world, then you can say that you have applied your discipline to life.

If you are a woman, you are expected to increase your depth of kindness and become loved by more people as a result of learning the Truth and attaining enlightenment. This would be out of the question if you live a life that is out of balance.

The same applies to young men. If you have been living an honest life, but somehow after studying the Truth you stray to become stuck up and corrupt, then you cannot know why you have learned Buddha's Truth.

This is true even for older people. If they become self-satisfied and begin to boast, it will be meaningless. Spiritual discipline will not be of value unless you become humbler and gentler, unless you become someone who is loved by others and at the same time can give love to others as you advance.

The Right Effort I teach at Happy Science is not like certain Buddhist practices, such as making the "Thousand-Day Circumambulation" [one-thousand-day journey in the mountains on foot], practicing religious austerities under a waterfall, or cramming a lot of knowledge of Buddha's Truth and then boasting about it. The knowledge is only material, and if the study of Buddha's Truth does not cause Light to shine in everyday life, it is completely useless. That is what I mean by Right Effort.

So, I would like to say:

Demonstrate the Truth, the knowledge you have learned, in actual life.

If your enlightenment is real, put it into practice.

You only have to look around to see if enlightenment is being practiced.

You only need to see how other people treat you to know that.

And keep an attitude of examining yourself to see if your character continues to improve.

Right Effort is not for creating a special kind of person immersed in Buddha's Truth. On the contrary, I would like you to become a more wonderful, more accomplished person than you have ever been, as a result of encountering Buddha's Truth, changing yourself, opening your mind, endeavoring for self-improvement, and overcoming your shortcomings.

And while doing so, never forget how difficult it is to maintain enlightenment. Do not make the mistake of thinking that you have attained enlightenment just by standing in its doorway. Do not forget that this is just the beginning of the real challenge of enlightenment.

For more information on Right Effort as the right way of making efforts, please refer to my books, including *Rojin, Buddha's Mystical Power.*

Chapter 8

Right Will

Lecture given on January 28, 1989
at Happy Science Training Hall, Tokyo

1

Proactive Self-Reflection to Open One's Future — Right Will

Self-reflection involves not only repentance for past deeds but also the planting of seeds for future development

In this chapter, I would like to discuss Right Will. The meaning of Right Will may not be so clear to you. Having read some books on Buddhism, I have the impression that no one really understands the meaning of Right Will; its essence has not been fully grasped. Preoccupied with the superficial meaning of words, authors have not really delved into the real meaning of Right Will.

That is because those who have written about Right Will have no actual experience of how "the effect of the mind" works. Even if they speak about the Eightfold Path or try to explain Right Thought or Right Will, because they have not actually experienced the mind's functions, they cannot be really sure what it all means.

Actually, you may not understand what I am talking about by simply hearing what I say. It is only by trying to put it into practice and experiencing it firsthand that you will understand.

What I am going to say about Right Will will be a departure from traditional Buddhist self-reflection. This is because the True

Eightfold Path contains more positive aspects than the traditional way self-reflection has been explained in Buddhism. As I have mentioned briefly in *The Essence of Buddha*, *The Laws of the Sun*, and others, I generally explain the concept of Right Will with more focus on a "mindset positioned for the future." Without this way of thinking, it is not possible to connect self-reflection to progress, both of which are part of the Fourfold Path, or to teach the idea of progress based on self-reflection.

If self-reflection is only limited to "repentance for past deeds," it will not lead to the idea of progress based on self-reflection. Rather, in the act of self-reflection, the "sprout of progress" must be included.

As you continue on in Right View, Right Thought, Right Speech, Right Action, Right Living, and Right Effort, you will deepen your self-reflection to give clarity to your mind and remove any impurity that shrouds it. Upon completion of this practice, you need to lay down a stepping stone for the future. You will find the critical turning point with Right Will, the seventh step in the Eightfold Path.

Creating utopia through Right Will

If you consider the connection between Right Will and love, the first path of the Fourfold Path, the essential point is having an active relationship with others. It is there that you find the connection between Right Will and love.

Your "will" is something you emit from inside yourself that radiates out. So you will have some involvement in other people's lives, if only minimally. There will always be an impact on others.

Therefore, thinking about the nature and content of one's "will" would have a great deal to do with creating utopia. Do not forget this.

It can be said that the concept of self-reflection contains essential elements to positively create the future – regarding society, the country, and human relationships.

2

The Materialization of Will

Will has physical power

I would like to add more detail to the analysis of Right Will. First of all, what exactly is "will"? Many thoughts flow in and out of the human mind. Some thoughts produce strong images, or rather they present themselves with very strong mental images.

Also, there are times when the mind may halt on a certain point and maintain focus on it. For example, if someone were to concentrate on me, I could really see his or her face. And I would think, "That person is thinking something about me." It really does happen.

In this way, if you focus on a person for more than a certain amount of time, that thought will surely be relayed to the other person. Both good and bad thoughts can equally be passed to another. Concentrated thoughts have such physical power, but most people are not very sensitive to them, so they cannot be sensed so clearly.

Focused thoughts toward a person can take on a physical form

So, what does it mean to project your face when you concentrate your thoughts on a person?

In a spiritual message of the German philosopher Emmanuel Kant, for example, he pointed out, "Here is a Kant drinking coffee. There is a Kant milking a cow." In a sense, he was showing that it is possible to divide our presence into multiple beings or create alter egos by concentrating our thoughts. In the above example, even if a person was not physically present, I could still see him or her in front of me.

This is an extremely interesting phenomenon. At such times, it is not that the soul of the person has slipped out, but rather that the concentration of thought came to be actualized.

It is possible in this world, but when we return to the other world, such focused thoughts will appear more clearly. In the world of spirits, when you focus your thought on a person, that person's image will appear within a moment. You will be able to interact with the person's image, but considering whether the actual being is there, in fact, it is not. This is really strange.

Such an effect also works to some extent in this three-dimensional world. Thus, such focused thoughts would affect many different people.

In fact, this is the true nature of what has been referred to since ancient times as *ikiryo*, or a living spirit, in Japanese classics such as *The Tale of Genji*. When you study the classics, you may think, "Well, that would be the kind of subject matter for an author from ancient times." However, when a person's thoughts become focused, they can appear in the form of a figure. This is certainly true.

In this way, one's concentrated thoughts, or "will," can always have some effect on others and one's future.

3

Right Will Is the Power to Create Happiness

Changing one's mind and changing the world through self-innovation

Now, let us think further about the nature of the "will" itself. To understand the meaning of "will" correctly is most important to create happiness for human beings.

Even if the first six paths of the Eightfold Path preceding Right Will are practiced correctly, Right Will can be quite difficult. If you cannot get the essential point of Right Will, you cannot really create happiness. You may get caught in a cycle of making mistakes and recovering from losses over and over. If you live in this way, it will be difficult to live a positive life.

I have stated many times that if you change your mind, the world will change. Also, with regard to the activities of Happy Science, I never say, "If you just gather here, you will become happy." I say, "If you join Happy Science, innovate yourself, and change your mind, then you will become happy. I will give you clues, but it is up to each individual to grasp them or not."

Therefore, if you think of Happy Science as merely a refuge or a place to escape from life, it is out of the question. Because this is a battlefield. It is a place that requires intense self-improvement. It is a place that demands a struggle with yourself. If you think, "If I just go to the place where this signboard is, I will be blessed and happy," it is not quite right. While you may not be successful in your work life or school life, if you come to Happy Science with the expectation of receiving benefits to become happy, it will not necessarily happen.

This is not a place of refuge, but a battlefield, because the voices from the high spirits that tell you to achieve self-innovation pour down like arrows, one after another. It is very difficult to survive the rain of arrows and remain intact. You are compelled to examine and change yourself in various ways.

If you fail to make this self-innovation, you will not be able to unlock your future potential.

Let me expand on this with a specific case.

The turning point where I transformed myself from a "sensitive literary youth" to a "god of fortune"

I often speak in front of people, and when I look at myself in the mirror, I find it intriguing that my face is gradually becoming more rounded and radiant, leading me to think that a god of fortune might be my soul sibling.

Thinking about why this has come about, it can be due to good nutrition, but it is not just because of material reasons. Indeed, there was a spiritual turning point somewhere in the history of my life.

When I look back on the years before I opened my spiritual pathway, I can truthfully say I was extremely sensitive.

Many of you would not believe it seeing me now, but I used to be so sensitive that something someone would say could remain in my mind for years. Even two or three years after the utterance, I still would have feelings of embarrassment, frustration, or disappointment. Such feelings would prick me like the thorns of a rose, reminding me of the past as if they had just happened moments ago.

Moreover, I was happy about being a literary youth, and I thought that sensitivity was a good thing. There were times when I actually felt that there were many things cutting into my heart to make me bleed slowly. And there was a part of me that would think my youthful sensitivity and the sadness that ate into my soul had contributed to shaping my life into a piece of art.

Even after I opened my spiritual pathway, I may have become more sensitive, much more so than before. The emotions of various people are directly transmitted to me.

Consequently, while I could remove various clouds and shadows through self-reflection, I also began to see many of my own shadows and mistakes, and for a period of time, I could not free myself from this situation. The deeper I went into self-reflection, the more I was able to notice various points about myself that were hard to change.

4

Change the Direction of Your Will

Ask yourself, "In the end, do I want to make myself happy or not?"

However, I managed to change direction at some point. Receiving words from a spiritual being prompted me to make the realignment.

In short, I was questioned intensely. "What do you want, after all? Do you only live to blame yourself for your sins and evils and to remind yourself you are not good enough? What kind of life do you envision in your mind? Do you want to explore the future or not? Do you want to make others happy or not? Do you want to make yourself happy or not? Be clear about all that you want. That's the starting point," he said.

When I was confronted with these questions, I realized I had never thought about them clearly enough.

Do away with self-pity and seek to love others

When I reflected on my vulnerable heart, which was so sensitive, I found myself trapped in self-pity.

I think there are many people like this. I am sure many things go wrong for you, your failures, your shortcomings, and the like. In fact, there are a lot of people who almost always have such negative thoughts in their heads and wallow in self-pity. They have difficulty getting out of this downward spiral. If you always choose to surround yourself in self-pity and constantly feel sorry for yourself, you will never get out of it. In the spiral of self-pity, the person who feels so low cannot be happy, much less love others. You would be too preoccupied with yourself to have an interest in others.

Then, people may keep on wondering why they are so unhappy, but it is actually they who are forcing themselves into unhappiness. It means they have a self-pitying attitude.

At the subconscious level, this self-pitying feeling will work to drive you into an even more miserable situation. Then, you will find yourself in circumstances where others might say nasty things about you and victimize you.

With a self-pitying attitude, you will come to face such an environment. You can experiment and obtain these results. Try living in a self-deprecating way. At once, people will start to tease you a lot and make fun of you. It will just happen. Really, it is a natural, spontaneous reaction to your self-pity. You cannot blame others for the outcome. It is what happens when you have a tendency to embrace misery.

*Change the direction of your "will" and
break free from your tendency to cling to unhappiness*

I am talking about your "will." If your "will" is directed in the wrong direction, unless you alter it, you will have to live with the "unhappiness syndrome."

What kind of life do you hope to live right now? You should at least have a clear answer to this question. Unless the direction of people's "wills" are properly set, there will be a great number of people who go in the wrong direction.

No matter how much you try to help or encourage them, there is nothing you can do about those who are heading down the road to misfortune. People who embrace misery are beyond saving. Even God or Buddha cannot save such people.

It is because this matter follows the Laws of the Mind, and each person advances in the direction they want to go. It is how these laws work.

5

The Laws of Realizing Hope

1) Do you show your "desires" to realize your objectives wholeheartedly?

Knowing the difference between "wish" and "desire"

Now, I would like to talk about having hope for happiness.

This means that when you want something to happen, if it really occurs, then you will be happy. It would be nice if what you wanted was appropriate and could be realized, but in reality, things do not go the way you want. Even when you hope for something, it will not materialize so easily.

As a result, it is likely that thoughts of realizing your hopes may slip from your mind, even if you might come across a reference to them. You might think, "Those kinds of things only apply to someone special; they don't relate to me."

The difference between "to wish" and "to desire" is worth considering. You might say, "I wish something would be like this" or "I wish something would happen this way." On the other hand, "desire" has more emotional appeal. "To desire" is used to describe a situation you strongly want to happen, or rather, "It has to happen no matter what."

In fact, this is where the difference between "thought" and "will" in realizing hope shows more distinctly. Unless hope is intensified to become desire, it will not be realized.

Suppose you think, "I wish something would turn out this way," and send out thought waves in accordance with your wish. However, in this earthly world, there are all sorts of obstacles that can interfere with your wish, so when you come up against them, you may easily change your thinking.

Let us say a Mercedes-Benz car is heading in a certain direction and hits a rock. At that instance, the rock may move a little, but the car will not be able to continue on in a straight course. If it hits another rock, the car will go further off course.

In this way, if you wish for some outcome to happen, but you run into obstacles, the "outcome" will not happen. After hitting one or two such obstacles, people usually give up trying. This is how the majority of people would act.

However, when these "wishes" become "desires," they become something much stronger, like a tank. Imagine the rock blocking the path of a tank. If the rock cannot be pushed out of the way, you can fire the tank's cannon to blow it up to keep moving forward.

In this way, if you can make your wish stronger to be like the tank; it will come true, but if what you want remains like the Mercedes-Benz, you may hesitate going forward because you do not want to damage your car. In short, it has very much to do with your self-image.

Think about whether you truly want to be happy

So, if you want to be happy, you have to think about the image you have of yourself as you practice Right Will.

In this instance, if you imagine yourself to be a Mercedes-Benz, you cannot go straight and will veer off when you hit a rock because you want to avoid ruining the car. But if your self-image gets stronger and becomes like a tank, you can push the rock aside, or if the rock does not move, you can fire a shell at it to blast it away. If you manage to reach this point, there is no reason why you cannot find a way to deal with obstacles. Please think about such differences.

In other words, even if you want to be happy, you will never attain happiness if you just think on a superficial level. There are plenty of people who just hope in a shallow manner. On further observance, many of them seem to identify with the "Mercedes-Benz" and hate to get hurt. As such, the best thing for them would be to not get hit, so they run away to avoid getting hurt. While they hope to move on, they do not want to damage their "Mercedes-Benz" because it is too expensive, so they wander away.

2) Self-confrontation of those trapped by pride

Confront yourself when you are fearful of getting hurt and running away from problems

Considering exactly what gets hurt, it is usually that which is referred to as "pride." It is the pride of regarding yourself as a "luxury car." You want to move on, but you think, "It would be terrible if I got hurt." Then you start to avoid any confrontation and run away. First of all, you fear getting hurt by facing up to a problem. The easiest thing for you to do in a bad situation would be to avoid it and escape without even trying to confront it.

You think you "want" something but end up running away from it. Probably about 70% of people have this kind of tendency, possibly more than that. There are actually so many people of this type, and that is basically the way it is.

Practicing positive thinking with seriousness

Then, what can be done to strengthen your wish to become like a "tank"?

Primarily, one must use positive thinking. If you incorporate positive thinking into methods of self-reflection, it will align with Right Will. That is where positive thinking can be integrated.

However, many people will have difficulty practicing positive thinking once they decide to do so. Their efforts fail to bring any results when their hopes end at the "wish" stage and do not proceed any further. If they push on, being determined to get through the situation at any cost, then a path will be found. However, in most cases, they will fall short. They will then begin to doubt their ability and gradually retreat into embracing misery again.

You must take positive thinking seriously if you want to put it into practice in real situations. You have to exert your utmost effort to practice it. If you only think about positive thinking or simply speak of it, you will completely forget about it when confronted with real-life problems and just evade them. This is the most probable outcome.

So, if you really want to put positive thinking into practice, you cannot do it unless you exert yourself seriously. It is not the time to worry about your pride. All you have to do is to be clear about what you want to achieve. If you are determined to realize your goal, you must do it with all your strength.

If you falter in this determination, you will likely be rebuffed by obstacles or avoid them. As a result, many people will revert to their former lifestyles, as if they loved living in ramshackle houses.

3) Ask yourself if you really want to serve the world as a child of God in a wholehearted manner

So, how can you strengthen your thoughts to the level of "desire"? This is an important point.

How can you obtain the desire that comes from the deepest part of your heart? How can you obtain the desperate desire to realize a goal at any cost? This has much to do with the goals and ideals you have. The question is, "What exactly are your ideals?"

If you are living without any particular goal, like a leaf floating on a pond, you will rarely go far. In contrast, if you have an ardent desire, as if a torrent were forcing everything out of its way, then you will be more likely to attain your ideals.

This is where you are really tested on whether you have trust in yourself, whether you really think you are a child of God, or whether you believe you have a solid core like a diamond deep inside. Those who consider themselves inadequate will never be able to achieve self-realization through the practice of Right Will.

In the end, it is a question of whether you deeply feel that you want to be of great service to the world.

If you cannot find such a desire within yourself, you must have lived a kind of life where you were given everything you needed by those around you. Reflect on this. If that is the case, you must have lived as if on charity. You have benefited from the kindness of others, but remain unsatisfied and still complain, claiming that it was not enough. This would be the kind of person who is very likely to have been on the receiving end of generous favors, a taker.

But truthfully, if you cannot find any desire to want to live for others and give something in return from the depth of your heart, it will not be good enough. You are in fact expected to have such honest desires. Only then will you be able to live a powerful life.

4) *Do not try to bind others with the power of your will*

Furthermore, in self-realization, it is not enough just to be as strong as a tank. There is another issue to consider, and that is the direction.

As the energy of your will functions to make things realized, it may do so even if it is pointed in the wrong direction. Therefore, direction is extremely important.

There is something I really want you to think about when you attempt to realize your goals using your will: You should never try to restrict others with the energy of your will. Do not ever think about forcefully changing someone else's life in order to make your life easier. This is the wrong attitude.

It is not appropriate to set goals for yourself while thinking, "I can't attain these goals unless that person acts in such and such a way." Do not be mistaken. This will turn your "will" into harm.

This type of self-realization can lead to Hell if something goes wrong. Even if there was nothing particularly wrong, the better result would be to return to the Rear Heaven in the Spirit World. You would be led to either of these two realms. This is very straightforward. If you make others unhappy as the result of your own self-realization, you will have to go to Hell. Those who have paved their way by using their "will" to change others for their own advantage will have to go to the rear part of Heaven, if not Hell.

Why would this happen? Because there is no love in these situations; there is a lack of love for others in these efforts at self-realization.

This is the love of oneself, not true love that gives, or altruistic love. Such people might even be appreciated by others for their actions, but the end results for these kinds of tendencies will lead them into the realm of the long-nosed *tengu* goblins or the realm of hermits in the rear part. As you can see, the direction you will go is divided into the front or rear section of the Spirit World.

The front side of the Spirit World is the place for people who truly self-actualize for the good of others, but the rear side is for those who ardently seek to show off. Consequently, these people will enter the realm of the psychic and supernatural in a variety of forms; it is a destination where unlimited self-love is manifested. Do not make this mistake.

6

Practicing Right Will

Consider the issues of "means, method, and timing" in achieving your goals

So what can you do to achieve certain goals?

For example, suppose that you expect to start a new business project with someone working in another organization. His section chief may say okay, seeming to have a good feeling about the project, but the general manager may object. In this case, if you try to forcibly persuade the general manager or wish for him to be demoted if he maintains his refusal, this will be unacceptable.

How should you consider such a situation as a good human being? This is the most important point concerning Right Will.

For a goal to become clear and defined, there are three conditions that give it shape, namely "means, method, and timing." However, it is very difficult to satisfy all the conditions.

Of course, there are people who clearly define means, method, and timing to realize their goals and take decisive action to eventually achieve success. However, such people already have a certain level of competence. If you have experienced success in the past and have an 80 to 90 % probability to achieve it, then you might act decisively to realize your goals. On the other hand, you will usually fail if you are full of doubt or fear, even if you try hard.

This is where the issues of "means, method, and timing" are relevant. In my book *Rojin, Buddha's Mystical Power*, I wrote in greater detail on these issues, and in fact they are key in considering spiritual self-realization.

A specific example of spiritual self-realization — my search for an ideal house

It may not be easy to understand if I talk about this theme too abstractly, so I will be more specific about a real-life example of hope fulfillment.

As a religious teacher, I read and study many different subjects extensively, so I need a certain amount of storage space to keep my books. From the time I started Happy Science, I felt that the house I was living in was very cramped.

It was probably in August of 1988 that a high spirit said to me, "You are working very hard, so we will help you to move into a bigger house."

By the following month, I had found a house that was about the size I needed. It was a fairly large house with a garden and conveniently located for work, so I was rather excited.

However, as the arrangements proceeded, the owner started to express some reservations. The landlord would not say exactly what the problem was, but it seemed to be about what he had learned about me. He was concerned because I was the head of an organization, which somehow seemed to cause him alarm. If that was the case, then I had no choice. It would not make sense to put pressure on the owner and try to force him to lease the house to me. Even if high spirits work hard to make arrangements, there is also the free will of people on earth. If the owner thought our group was somewhat alarming, then that would be the end of the story. So, I simply accepted the situation and thought about finding another property.

Then, the following month, another potential residence was found. This time, the location was even better than the previous house.

I like places with good scenery where I can meditate or contemplate at night. And the second house was located in a neighborhood with a large park. So when I went to take a look at it, I thought, "This is great!"

It was a combination of two living units. Perhaps the owner thought the whole building was too large to be leased by a single family, so he split the house into two and planned to lease them as separate units. It had a back yard with trees and a large park nearby, so I was delighted and proceeded to make arrangements to lease it.

However, there was a problem — the owner of the house was a professor of applied physics at one of Japan's national universities and a fervent materialist, so to speak. In my interview with him, we had a short conversation. As a doctor of science, he did not have the slightest belief in spirits, making the conversation not so friendly or pleasant. So I thought, "Well, this will not work."

But the month after that, another housing possibility became available.

A few days prior, I had dreamt of a triangular house with a lot of diamonds on it; then, this next choice appeared.

It turned out to be a house with a lot of glass windows, and I found it to be the best of the three candidates. I was surprised because it was big, had a garden, was close to a park, and most importantly, the rent was reasonable. The rent was about half of what the previous properties were asking.

Later, I managed to have a lot of bookshelves installed in the house to accommodate around 15,000 books [my library of thirty years ago]. It turned out to be the choice that most satisfied all the conditions I had.

The total search period was about two months. I started looking for a house in September and decided in November, taking two months to find a house.

About a month after signing the contract for the third house, the professor from the national university mentioned earlier approached me to plead with me to lease his house. He said, "I've done some research about you and found out that the books you have written seem to be selling really well, so now I'd like to do business with you." I thought to myself, "Don't bother, it's too late!" The owner had changed his mind and tried to lease his house to me, saying, "I'll give you a great discount on the rent, so please reconsider leasing my house," but he had already missed his chance.

The place I finally leased was cheaper, larger, and roomier. If I had leased the professor's property, which was a combination of two living units, it would have been inconvenient because I was thinking of using one of them as a library. The house that became available later was much more convenient. It was a rather intricate story, but it actually happened.

The university professor regretted that he had been disrespectful to me, but I had expected that would happen.

When I first met the professor, I knew instinctively that he was a subscriber of the *Mainichi Shimbun* daily newspaper. In December, the paper carried advertisements for my books four days in a row with the caption, "Over 1.2 million copies sold!" I was expecting that after seeing the ads, he would come to ask me to lease his house.

The advertisements were a month late in coming out; they had originally been planned for November. Most probably, I could have rented his house if the ads had come out as planned. But due to some mistake by the editorial staff, the advertisements were delayed by a month, so it followed that I did not lease the professor's house.

In the end, it turned out to be a better result because I could move into a much better place that appeared later.

Now, Happy Science has built Taigokan [Sacred Shrine of Great Enlightenment] and other Master's holy temples.

7

Accumulation While Waiting

In self-realization,
turn your thoughts firmly toward God

The example of the house I just mentioned shows very clearly how spiritual self-realization works.

First of all, it happens according to the concept that certain opportunities will be provided. In the process of a concept being realized in the earthly realm, it gradually becomes more and more concrete. What was flowing fluidly like lava begins to solidify.

In the process, something like rock starts to form. This is the well-known "free will" of people on earth. It is possible for it to form and affect the flow of lava.

The lava will eventually settle and take form, and the initial concept will solidify as planned or in some different manner.

If the person's thoughts are firmly oriented toward God, it will result in a better form. If his or her thoughts are not strong enough, the concept may be realized in a somewhat lower-quality outcome. This is what can happen.

Be one with God and continue to make efforts without forcing a specific time frame

Concerning the three houses I mentioned earlier, if I had used my free will and insisted, "The first place is the best, so I will definitely take it no matter what," what would have happened? In spite of the owner's concern about the reputation of our religious group, what would have happened if I had said, "No, we are not a religion but a group based on science," in order to influence him to lease the property to me? What if I had tried my best to persuade him by offering to pay rent that was ¥100,000 more than he was asking for? At that point, I might have possibly gotten the house, since I would have had no idea about the properties that would become available later. However, I instantly shifted my attention and thought, "There will certainly be another choice."

The results followed as described above. The time it took for my hope to be realized was only about two months.

As you can see, the "time" factor cannot be exactly determined as the flow of time on earth is somewhat different than it is in heaven. Also, the background conditions may vary to some extent.

However, if you have a really strong desire that is in tune with God, you can eventually expect good results. This bond with God is really important.

I have shown a case of self-realization using my own experience. As you can see, it is important to have a strong conviction that things will turn out positively, and that a path will be opened. In the meantime, you need to keep advancing without retreating and not limit yourself with a preset time frame. In the process, if you keep making efforts that you think are necessary, then you will always find a way forward.

You should not hesitate because of any initial snags and become disheartened. If you waver here, you will never truly achieve self-realization. First, be confident and stay grounded. Then, if you can believe that your wishes will definitely be realized, they will surely happen.

Stay grounded and accumulate basic knowledge and experiences

The same could be said about the founding of Happy Science. I had to wait about five or six years until I finally started Happy Science. The fact that it took so long to begin serious activity may have seemed deliberate, but it took me that period of time to study and gain experience.

However, going through such a period can be very frustrating and make you impatient because although the direction is already shown you cannot advance. Although the rails had already been laid, running at the speed of a bullet train was not yet possible, and running on a slow train can be frustrating. It is hard even if you know that you will always move forward.

This is the most critical point in practicing Right Will. This is when perseverance is needed; I think it is important to have an attitude of being firmly grounded but moving forward slowly and carefully while building up reserves.

As you draw up plans based on what you have accumulated during the initial slow period, you can gather speed to realize your goals and make up for the delay.

After all, setting the foundation is very important. As with judging things or anything else, without basic knowledge and experience, it is difficult to grasp the essence of things. On the other hand, if you have these resources, very good development can be expected.

A path will open up if you stop thinking negatively about yourself and have a cheerful disposition

So far, I have described the general idea of Right Will; whether or not you follow the path correctly will bring you to the fork in your journey leading toward happiness or misery.

Therefore, you should first check to see if your thoughts and feelings are consistently self-negating or self-punishing, or if you have a tendency to accuse or wish harm to others.

Unless you have a cheerful disposition, you will never find a path forward. You can never expect to be happy if you constantly have thoughts like the following: "I'm really not good enough";

"I'm stupid"; "I've done a lot of bad things in the past"; "I always make mistakes"; and "I am ugly, dim-witted, have no talent, and all these can't be helped." That kind of thinking should be done away with and instead be replaced with positive statements such as the following: "I'm loved by God"; "I cannot be miserable when I'm studying so much at Happy Science"; and "I need just a little more patience, so I'll keep doing my best." Then a path will surely open up. This is when you have to work really hard.

You must replace what is in your mind and fill yourself with positivity and a cheerful disposition.

Similarly, there is absolutely no way to be happy by hating others. You will never become happy if you feel resentment, envy, jealousy toward others, so strive to abandon such tendencies.

8

The Importance of Forgetting

Value the technique of forgetting

Here is one important truth.

It is that in order to become truly able to practice Right Will, the use of "forgetting" is also an important technique. It is very important to value this.

If you become caught up over certain recurring thoughts, being bound by them actually prevents you from self-realization.

Therefore, value the technique of forgetting. This is also an important virtue.

Forgetting does not mean disposing of the bad things and remembering only the things that are convenient to you. Rather, it is also an "act of love" to forget, for example, words that others have said that have troubled you.

Upon self-reflection, forgive yourself and quickly change your thinking

After all, it is also important to forgive yourself.

You can reflect on past thoughts and deeds, but they cannot be changed. You cannot cancel what has already been done. If you think you have tried to make amends to the fullest of your thoughts and deeds, then you should forgive yourself as well. This is also important.

What you should do in these situations is to try to better your life with more merit from then on. It is not just about filling in the holes you have dug in the past, or making up for what you did before. Once you have done what was necessary, I recommend that you decide to atone for your past mistakes by living a more positive life.

Those who fail to adopt this technique of properly forgetting will fail in their effort to follow Right Will.

In other words, it is about quickly changing your attitude or outlook. People who are slow to change their mental attitudes will let unhappiness drag on. Once an irreversible bad situation has occurred, it could be possible to compensate for it by producing good achievements in the future. Good acts, or good deeds, will always spread to affect other people. If you cannot undo a deed from the past, why not pay it back five times, or ten times instead? Then your debt will be offset.

Again, please remember the importance of the skill of forgetting.

Suggesting the virtue of forgetting to those who cannot forget past misfortunes

Take note that this especially pertains to women since many of them have difficulty in forgetting.

It would be good for a woman to have a good memory for studying, but instead there is a tendency for them to have an extremely good emotional memory. This is not helpful because it gives rise to unhappiness. The logic such a woman might use is, "You said kind words of love to me then, but now none at all. I cannot accept this."

A wife may complain to her husband, saying things like this: "When you proposed to me, you gave me such good compliments..."; "You said I'm the best wife in the country"; or "You told me I'm a good cook, but now you say my food is terrible." I would guess there are many husbands whose wives make comments like this: "You are the worst," "What you did is unforgivable as a human being," and the like.

This shows that their selective memories tend to be negative, a direction that makes them really unhappy.

So, if you are having trouble with someone with a very good memory, I recommend that you suggest to that person the importance of forgetting. You can advise, "Forgetting is a prerequisite for becoming a great person." Then the person may gradually learn not to expect words of praise so that everyday moods will be calmer.

This is particularly so for a husband whose wife has a good memory. If he does not manage to help her make efforts to forget things, she may hold grudges for a long time.

I think it is important to advise that "forgetting is a great virtue." At least, you may be able to influence an unsettled wife.

After all, not being able to forget is one of the causes of unhappiness. Selective memory that works to produce too much misery is not good, so it is better to forget. Some women have a tendency to think about particular things for a long time and end up tormenting themselves, so it is much better to learn to forget certain things at the time they occur.

Basically, my recommendation for husbands is to practice positive thinking. This means to make efforts to encourage the spouse to forget bad past situations and focus on hopes for the future, telling her things such as "The future will be better." That way, the atmosphere at home will be more amicable.

Here, I have talked about Right Will.

In some Buddhist traditions, Right Will is interpreted as meaning "correct memory," and the question is asked whether one has accurately memorized the teachings of Buddha. This can be a useful practice in connection to Right Meditation, which is the subject of the next chapter.

Chapter 9

Right Meditation

正
定

Lecture given on January 28, 1989
at Happy Science Training Hall in Tokyo

1

Serenity Within Is the First Step to Happiness

Let me talk about Right Meditation. There is an extremely difficult part of Right Meditation, because in this worldly dimension, neither the method nor the verification of its results and effects have been sufficiently established. This is because the questions of "how one begins meditation" and "what should be the result" are left to each person's experience and cannot be adequately tracked. In that sense, these are extremely difficult aspects of meditation.

I would now like to emphasize why there is Right Meditation in the Eightfold Path. I would like to point out that "meditating rightly" is actually a technique to attain happiness. A cause of unhappiness can be that your mind is unsettled and disturbed by frustration or insecurity.

Stability of the mind is more important than you might think. No one is happy when his or her mind is disturbed or develops a dizzying stream of thought. It is a miserable state.

Therefore, if your mind appears very transparent and calm when someone inquires about the state of your mind, then at least you would have taken the first step to happiness. On the other hand, if your mood is in constant upheaval, if your thoughts cannot focus, if you cannot sleep at night because your mind is troubled, then unfortunately you have fallen into a state of unhappiness.

So, what would be the best way to control or calm your mind when it is disturbed like churning water? Related to this question, I have referred to the "pointer needle of the mind" before.

The human mind is, in a sense, like one of the pointer hands on a clock. When the mind is disturbed, it can be described as a pointer needle that is pointed downward and swinging like a pendulum. You need to have it change direction so that it slowly rotates upward like a metronome.

What would be necessary to do this? So far, I have mainly discussed inner issues – what is in your mind or what you are thinking. However, Right Meditation uses approaches to the mind by external means as well. In other words, you try to restore your state of mind by using nonmental techniques.

2

Start Self-Reflection by Breathing Exercises

Using harmonized breathing,
your state of mind becomes peaceful, letting light come in

To be more specific, it is natural to start with breathing exercises. By regulating your breathing, any irregularity or irritation of the mind will subside.

This holds true as a countermeasure against evil spirits. Considering what to do when an evil spirit approaches, one thing that works effectively is breathing exercises. As you take a deep breath of air and continue to focus on breathing for a while, what is irritating the mind will disappear and the mind will become more peaceful. Also, as you control your breathing, Light will enter. It is rather intriguing, but this happens when you practice this method.

Another idea is to carefully "breathe before you get angry." If you take a breath before cursing or getting angry, your fury will subside. I wonder if you have ever experienced this. As you raise your fist, if you were made to take a deep breath and actually breathe deeply, your anger would become subdued. Such a mysterious phenomenon can occur, and it should also be considered one of the mercies. You are given a way to control and harmonize your mind through breathing.

And breathing has a more positive meaning than just harmonizing the mind. That is, "harmonizing the mind through breathing induces the needle of the mind to point toward the heavenly realm."

When you cannot think clearly,
try to practice deep breathing

Some people may not be good at self-reflection or have difficulty in clearing their minds. If you are one of them, you probably breathe just by inhaling and exhaling using your throat and lungs. But by focusing on your belly when you inhale and allowing more air to come deep down, you will be able to think more clearly.

Therefore, when you have difficulty in self-reflection, try to do deep breathing exercises, focusing on your belly. When you breathe in and out deeply for a few moments, distractions and anxiety will be reduced.

If you are not able to practice self-reflection, there is a possibility that you may be possessed by an evil spirit. But even though it may not be an evil spirit, if your mind is constantly filled with unsettled thoughts, there would be a confusion of things coming out of your head, like bubbles. This forms a thin film of sorts that has to be removed. Distracting thoughts are buzzing around your head, so you need to dispel them. The breathing exercises are one of the most effective ways to do this.

Breathing affects blood circulation and increases the amount of oxygen inside the body. Physically speaking, the increased intake of oxygen allows the body to function better, and you can think more clearly. Breathing fresh air can indeed improve the clarity of your mind. These are physical conditions, but it is necessary to satisfy them.

3

Receiving Light from the Heavenly World

The depth of serenity that you can achieve through breathing exercises is closely related to "how high in the spiritual dimension you can attune to."

Those who are well-practiced at meditation can control their minds after very brief breathing exercises. They become noticeably much calmer. As you advance further in meditation, you will be able to clear away distracting thoughts in just two or three breaths. I would like you to aim to achieve this level, if possible.

However, there is a time when breathing exercises alone may not be enough for you to control your mind to concentrate. It is when you are extremely physically tired. If you are in this condition, breathing exercises alone will not be enough. If it is mild physical fatigue, you can gradually become clear-headed as you continue your breathing, but in the case of extreme fatigue, you cannot expect good results. In such cases, you need to think about resting your body. It is a good idea to rest your body first and then try to control your mind to concentrate through breathing exercises.

What would be the result of attaining serenity within? You would be able to receive the Light from the heavenly world. This is very straightforward. When your mind is calm and centered, the

Light comes in. The result of receiving the Light is that your own personality brightens up.

Have you ever met someone who was looking pale or unhealthy, but began to perk up as you began to talk to this person? I have experienced this many times, and on those occasions the Light was flowing in. The worries in their minds dissolved, and their frustrations and turbulence came under control. Furthermore, their guardian spirits would send them signals. On such occasions, people's faces brighten up in delight. It might be an overstatement to say that they had "stars in their eyes," but that is the kind of mood they may experience.

4

Becoming One with God or Buddha

Right Meditation is about trying to become one with God or Buddha

Next, I would like to give more detail about Right Meditation. As a member of Happy Science, what exactly should you do, or how can you attain Right Meditation?

First of all, I would like you to confirm your basic stance; it is the act of infinitely striving to become one with God or Buddha.

Right Meditation is not about attempting to seek a space where you are alone and isolated. Right Meditation is the act of trying to become one with God or Buddha. When you aim to achieve the state of infinitely being one with Him, you are actually aiming for the state of the Tathagata. This is the goal of Right Meditation.

You can choose a sitting posture and hand position that will help your meditation

With "becoming one with God or Buddha" in mind, what should you do in actual practice?

I do not want to be too specific about sitting posture or how you should put your hands together. This is because if you focus too much on style, you will be distracted by the details and become unable to concentrate on the substance. The most important thing is the mind, and style is merely a supporting factor. It is only an aid, so if you impose a difficult posture and style on yourself, you will be distracted and not make progress.

So, although the position may be different from person to person, I would suggest at least that you sit up straight.

Also, it would be good to find a posture that will allow you to breathe deeply. I recommend that the posture you use should allow you to inhale and exhale deeply without problem.

As for your leg placement, you can sit in the *seiza* style, kneeling with the knees together on the floor sitting with the legs folded under your torso, but if you cannot hold this position for long, you can sit cross-legged, or if you are a woman, you can sit with your legs folded to the side with one thigh on the floor.

Moreover, I just want to point out that if you slouch, it is very difficult to center your mind.

There are several ways of positioning the hands, each with its own meaning, but the most popular style is to put your hands together as in prayer. The praying-hands style forms the shape of an antenna, and in this style, you will become spiritually receptive. At the same time, spiritual light is emitted from your hands. The hands are where spiritual light comes out, and you may apply your hands to treat illness. The right hand especially is stronger in emitting spiritual currents. The hands always are where the spiritual current flows out.

By putting your hands together, a "magnetic field" is thereby created. When you put your hands together in prayer and point your fingertips upward, you are sending out a broadcast signal, so to speak. This initiates the effect of creating spiritual contact, and invites spiritual response. Thus, the praying-hands style is the most popular.

Where does one position one's praying hands? This also depends on the style. There is a style to raise the praying hands up to the mouth, but the drawback is that this posture cannot be maintained for long. Therefore, I recommend you to position your hands in front of your chest. This is a way to focus on communication or interaction with spirits.

However, if you would like to focus on self-reflection, keeping your hands raised may also cause somewhat of a problem. After a period of time, you will become distracted in keeping your hands raised and will have difficulty deepening your self-reflection.

At that time, you may release your praying hands and place them lightly on your lap. Some yoga practitioners put their hands palm up in their laps, but in this position, people usually have difficulty concentrating, so palms can be faced downward. You can choose a position you can relax in.

In the end, it is about finding the right posture that makes it easier for you to center your mind. The truth is that there is no required posture. Lying down is acceptable. Standing on your head is possible, too. Even when in the bath it is actually alright. However, it is hard for one to feel that one is meditating without a proper appearance, so you need to find some particular position to set yourself apart from ordinary activities. Using this particular mode of meditation will be a way to create a partition from your everyday life.

5

The Happy Science Style of Right Meditation

First, recite "The True Words Spoken By Buddha" and then start practicing centering meditation

Now, I would like to make some suggestions for practicing Right Meditation with Happy Science. First of all, it is necessary to harmonize your spiritual wavelength, so I would like you to breathe deeply for a while, and after that, if possible, recite "The True Words Spoken By Buddha" [Happy Science's basic sutra]. This will not take more than ten minutes. Then, if you would like to do self-reflection, this would be the right time. You can start self-reflection based on the Eightfold Path, following the practical guidelines which I have explained in this book.

If you would like to pray, I would suggest you use Happy Science's prayer books or the "Prayer to El Cantare."

How much time set aside for these spiritual practices will vary from person to person. Taking too much time, however, would make the effort less effective. It should not be a one-time event, so you can set aside time according to your daily schedule. If you are extremely busy, it will be difficult to set aside much time, so I think it is best to keep the amount of time to shorter periods that you can fit in as a part of your daily routine without too much time conflict. It would be fine to set aside fifteen to thirty minutes every day for such spiritual practices.

"The True Words Spoken By Buddha" is created by Buddha's life force and embodies the Light with extremely strong vibrations

I suggested earlier to begin by reciting "The True Words Spoken By Buddha." The reason for this is because it is a sutra comprised of *kotodama*, or words having spiritual power, and therefore it has Light with extremely strong vibrations. All the words in this sutra have this quality. The sutra is composed of regular words, but the sound of each word and the way it is arranged make a difference and produce a rhythm of Light. Just like a musical chord, the arrangement of the words creates a signal that is sent to the heavenly world. When I look with my spiritual eye at a person who is reciting "The True Words Spoken By Buddha," I can clearly see spheres of light coming out of his or her mouth.

Reciting this sutra has such strong power that it works to ward off evil spirits to some extent, and also to clear away evil or disharmonious thoughts. It is a good idea to first clear away these negative influences before starting meditation. Entering into a centering meditation while possessed by an evil spirit or the like is dangerous. I would like to draw your attention to this kind of risk.

My suggestion at this point is for you to make it a habit of reciting "The True Words Spoken By Buddha" before starting on centering meditation.

As you might know, "The True Words Spoken By Buddha" is comprised of words reflecting Buddha's life force. Therefore, by reciting this sutra, you will attract the central Light of Happy Science, and you will be empowered. While Happy Science has a wide variety of teachings, at its heart there is still the spirit of Buddhism. Therefore, by reciting "The True Words Spoken By Buddha," a pathway is formed that connects to the central Light. Reciting this sutra has such an ability.

Do not try to choose too many subjects when you practice self-reflection, but focus on them one by one

When you practice self-reflection, do not choose too many subjects or details, but focus on each one at a time. It is a good idea to first concentrate on one path, for example, Right Speech, Right View, and so on, and then further narrow the range of subjects to reflect upon.

For example, you could focus on a particular time when you were most distressed, and reflect on what you thought and did at that time. This attitude is important. It is far better to do a little bit at a time than to be too ambitious and end up doing nothing.

When you are physically sick, choose to study the Truth instead of trying to practice centering meditation

I talked about practicing your centering meditation after reciting "The True Words Spoken By Buddha." However, this may be somewhat dangerous for those who are physically sick, those who obviously suffer from spiritual disturbance, or those who constantly suffer from delusions and are helpless because of the influence of spirits. What is recommended for these types of people is not practicing centering meditation, but other activities such as listening to one of my CDs of sutra recitations or lectures, watching a DVD of my lectures, or reading a book on the Truth. I would like you to concentrate your energy on these efforts to study the Truth. After your condition improves, you can start on centering meditation.

If spiritual phenomena begin to occur, you must then stop there and refrain from practicing meditation further. You must not rejoice over experiencing spiritual phenomena. Be aware of your state of mind and determine whether it is good or not. If you do not think you are in good condition and are experiencing spiritual phenomena, it is time to stop meditating. Gather courage and stop.

This chapter has been about the methods of Right Meditation.

Chapter 10

General Statement

*The Significance of the Eightfold Path
in Today's World*

Lecture given on January 28, 1989
at Happy Science Training Hall, Tokyo

What Is the Purpose of the True Eightfold Path?

Finally, as a general statement, I would like to summarize the methods of self-reflection.

To the questions, "Why do you need the True Eightfold Path? What is the purpose of the True Eightfold Path?" I would like to answer with three points.

1) Adapting the Eightfold Path to modern society

The first point in showing the significance of the True Eightfold Path is to address the current situation where the true spirit of the Eightfold Path taught by Shakyamuni Buddha has been lost over a time period spanning more than 2,500 years. It has been interpreted in various ways by Buddhist scholars, but its essence has remained unclear. Also, no answer has been provided to the questions of "How should we use the Eightfold Path?" and "What is its true meaning?"

Therefore, I have taught about the Eightfold Path, which can be referred to as the "secret treasure of mankind," in a way that can be applied to modern society in a practical manner. The Eightfold Path should not be teachings that are beyond the reach of people wanting to make use of them. The primary significance of the True Eightfold Path is to teach it clearly so that you can practice its principles.

2) The Eightfold Path as the goal of spiritual discipline

The second significant point of the True Eightfold Path is that it gives clear goals of spiritual discipline.

It may depend on how each individual defines the word "enlightenment," what one interprets it to mean. I would say that as far as enlightenment is concerned, it is without limit. It will never be possible to claim, "I have attained final enlightenment!" You may be able to stand at the gateway of enlightenment or maintain a certain level of enlightenment, but it is impossible to know whether you are actually enlightened or not until you return to the other world. Throughout your life, spiritual learning will continue as a process.

Therefore, when you think you have "achieved enough," that is the beginning of your downfall. Even if you have heightened your state of mind to a certain level, what happens after is different from person to person. As far as the level of a person's spiritual state is concerned, some people will continue to advance, others will only maintain the status quo, and still others will regress. If you take a particular year of someone's life and observe it objectively, there are always areas of progress and areas of regression.

In that sense, even for those who have currently attained a certain level in their state of mind, it is not promised that the same level can be maintained one month later. It would be much more difficult to assess their state of mind one year later.

To that end, Happy Science offers examinations to measure members' "enlightenment" to some extent, but this must not be misunderstood. Your achievement and state of mind at a given moment may be measured, but it will not remain the same if circumstances change.

You may experience a variety of incidents, and many different situations will occur throughout your life. Whether you will be able to remain in the exact same state will be subject to your spiritual discipline in the future. In order to overcome the challenges of each unforeseen incident or event, you are given the True Eightfold Path. Even if you have once attained enlightenment, it is not final.

Therefore, it is very important to apply the True Eightfold Path as you experience changing circumstances in order to remove any cloudiness or impurities from your mind. Then, as I mentioned in the chapter on Right Will, it is very important to make efforts in self-actualizing to create your right future. After all, you must continue to fight with all your might to maintain your state of mind as various phenomena occur in accordance with your position, role, and surroundings.

In that sense, practicing the True Eightfold Path will not end until you die, or until you complete your spiritual discipline in this earthly life, and perhaps it will continue even into your next life. The style may change somewhat, but I believe this practice will continue into your next incarnation.

Therefore, no matter how important a role you may have or how well you are evaluated by others, always be sure to practice self-reflection based on these eight aspects of the True Eightfold Path. These eight approaches of self-reflection are "safety valves," so to speak. They are guideposts to live by to prevent you from going astray.

3) The Eightfold Path as principles to create utopia

The third way the True Eightfold Path is significant is that it serves as principles to create utopia.

I have spoken on the theme of utopia on various occasions using these expressions: "from a small utopia to a great utopia" and "from a personal utopia to a public utopia." What do they mean?

First of all, the utopia that I refer to consists of two kinds of realms: One is the world of the mind, or the inner world, and the other is the world on earth where human beings live, or the external world. The creation of the "small utopia" or "personal utopia" begins with taking control of your own mind and resolutely protecting your kingdom within.

Therefore, creating utopia in your inner world through the practice of the True Eightfold Path will be the way to light up the outside world as well.

If seen with spiritual eyes from far above, the people whose vision has become clarified through the practice of the True Eightfold Path and who are receiving the Light of God or Buddha seem to beam with light, as if they are bright candles or lighthouses. They can appear as if Divine fire has set down in the many places where they are present. The entire landscape would be like an urban night view seen from above, as if a city set in complete darkness were to light up, with small lights randomly being turned on one by one.

I would like you to know that this is how everything begins. Creating a utopia within individual minds will be the starting point of making this world into a utopia. It is impossible to realize ideals in a sweep or achieve political reform, economic reform, or religious reform. You must not have the false illusion of a perfect system or an ideal environment. You must not expect that an ideal personage will bring you all you wish for, or that perfect circumstances will necessarily bring you happiness. Such modes of thinking are quite unrealistic.

Self-innovation to achieve true happiness in the name of enlightenment

Please light up the places where each of you are located as you bear your own challenges and problems. I would like you to know that the way to kindle your light is to simply follow the True Eightfold

Path. I hope that through the practice of the True Eightfold Path, you can light the wick of your candle or your lamp.

It is the responsibility of each of you to kindle your light. It is each person's job to let your lamp shine. I will teach you how to light a fire, but it is you who has to set it ablaze. If there is no flame, it is probably because you are not trying to start a fire.

The act of starting a flame is nothing but making efforts at self-innovation. Those who are not willing to change themselves, to turn their minds in the direction of the mind of God or Buddha, are not quite welcome at Happy Science.

Happy Science is not being run to serve those people. Happy Science shows you the right path and teaches you to follow in the right direction. However, as you follow in the right direction, it is the responsibility of each of you to light the wick of your lamp and make it shine.

Such efforts represent your true happiness in the name of "enlightenment."

AFTERWORD

Simply put, this book is the accumulation of methodologies with which to seek enlightenment in the modern age. By clearly revealing the proper manner of self-reflection, which is the main path of enlightenment, it also unveils the essence of Shakyamuni's Buddhism.

What exactly was Shakyamuni Buddha's Eightfold Path? The explanation I have presented will be helpful to both beginners and experts. As the author, I would be more than happy if you would keep this book within easy reach to help guide your daily spiritual discipline.

Ryuho Okawa
Master & CEO of Happy Science Group
March 1989

AFTERWORD TO THE
NEW AND REVISED EDITION

In this book, I have arranged the order of the Eightfold Path differently from in my first edition to conform to traditional Buddhism.

Specifically, I have gone back to the traditional sequence of Right Thought, Right Speech, Right Action, and so on.

In my first edition, I chose to put Right Speech first because in my current incarnation the enlightenment of Right Speech is where I myself started. However, for the purpose of learning Buddhism, I now think it would be better to keep the same order used in Shakyamuni Buddha's Eightfold Path.

Also, at the time of the original lectures, it had only been two and a half years since I quit my position at a trading company, so I found that my commentary was more business-oriented.

Therefore, this time I also added some comments summarizing relevant Buddhist teachings at the end of the chapters. If you have advanced in your studies, you may also focus on these additional comments.

I think it is rather difficult for modern people to understand the Eightfold Path, but with my current feelings, I would like to publish *The True Eightfold Path* again to appeal to the world.

Ryuho Okawa
Master & CEO of Happy Science Group
May 30, 2020

ABOUT THE AUTHOR

RYUHO OKAWA was born on July 7th 1956, in Tokushima, Japan. After graduating from the University of Tokyo with a law degree, he joined a Tokyo-based trading house. While working at its New York headquarters, he studied international finance at the Graduate Center of the City University of New York. In 1981, he attained Great Enlightenment and became aware that he is El Cantare with a mission to bring salvation to all humankind. In 1986, he established Happy Science. It now has members in over 140 countries across the world, with more than 700 local branches and temples as well as 10,000 missionary houses around the world. The total number of lectures has exceeded 3,250 (of which more than 150 are in English) and over 2,800 books (of which more than 550 are Spiritual Interview Series) have been published, many of which are translated into 31 languages. Many of the books, including *The Laws of the Sun* have become best sellers or million sellers. To date, Happy Science has produced 23 movies. The original story and original concept were given by the Executive Producer Ryuho Okawa. Recent movie titles are *Beautiful Lure–A Modern Tale of "Painted Skin"* (live-action movie scheduled to be released in May 2021), *Yume Handan soshite Kyoufu Taiken e* (literally: "The Interpretation of Dreams and Fearful Experience," live-action movie scheduled to be released in Summer of 2021), and *Uchu no Ho - Elohim hen -* (literally, "The Laws of the Universe - The Age of Elohim," animation movie scheduled to be released in Fall of 2021). He has also composed the lyrics and music of over 250 songs, such as theme songs and featured songs of movies. Moreover, he is the Founder of Happy Science University and Happy Science Academy (Junior and Senior High School), Founder and President of the Happiness Realization Party, Founder and Honorary Headmaster of Happy Science Institute of Government and Management, Founder of IRH Press Co., Ltd., and the Chairperson of New Star Production Co., Ltd. and ARI Production Co., Ltd.

WHAT IS EL CANTARE?

El Cantare means "the Light of the Earth," and is the Supreme God of the Earth who has been guiding humankind since the beginning of Genesis. He is whom Jesus called Father and Muhammad called Allah. Different parts of El Cantare's core consciousness have descended to Earth in the past, once as Alpha and another as Elohim. His branch spirits, such as Shakyamuni Buddha and Hermes, have descended to Earth many times and helped to flourish many civilizations. To unite various religions and to integrate various fields of study in order to build a new civilization on Earth, a part of the core consciousness has descended to Earth as Master Ryuho Okawa.

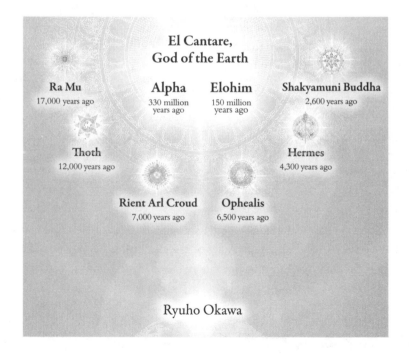

El Cantare,
God of the Earth

Ra Mu
17,000 years ago

Alpha
330 million
years ago

Elohim
150 million
years ago

Shakyamuni Buddha
2,600 years ago

Thoth
12,000 years ago

Hermes
4,300 years ago

Rient Arl Croud
7,000 years ago

Ophealis
6,500 years ago

Ryuho Okawa

Alpha is a part of the core consciousness of El Cantare who descended to Earth around 330 million years ago. Alpha preached Earth's Truths to harmonize and unify Earth-born humans and space people who came from other planets.

Elohim is a part of El Cantare's core consciousness who descended to Earth around 150 million years ago. He gave wisdom, mainly on the differences of light and darkness, good and evil.

Shakyamuni Buddha was born as a prince into the Shakya Clan in India around 2,600 years ago. When he was 29 years old, he renounced the world and sought enlightenment. He later attained Great Enlightenment and founded Buddhism.

Hermes is one of the 12 Olympian gods in Greek mythology, but the spiritual Truth is that he taught the teachings of love and progress around 4,300 years ago that became the origin of the current Western civilization. He is a hero that truly existed.

Ophealis was born in Greece around 6,500 years ago and was the leader who took an expedition to as far as Egypt. He is the God of miracles, prosperity, and arts, and is known as Osiris in the Egyptian mythology.

Rient Arl Croud was born as a king of the ancient Incan Empire around 7,000 years ago and taught about the mysteries of the mind. In the heavenly world, he is responsible for the interactions that take place between various planets.

Thoth was an almighty leader who built the golden age of the Atlantic civilization around 12,000 years ago. In the Egyptian mythology, he is known as god Thoth.

Ra Mu was a leader who built the golden age of the civilization of Mu around 17,000 years ago. As a religious leader and a politician, he ruled by uniting religion and politics.

"The True Words Spoken By Buddha"

This is one of the greatest gospels for humankind; this sutra, which is the English version of Happy Science's basic sutra, was written directly in English by Master Ryuho Okawa.

"THE TRUE WORDS SPOKEN BY BUDDHA"

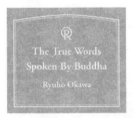

In this CD, Master Ryuho Okawa recites "The True Words Spoken By Buddha." Highly recommended to receive it together with the sutra book.

THE LECTURE ON "THE TRUE WORDS SPOKEN BY BUDDHA"

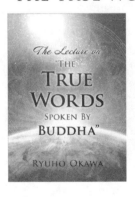

In this lecture, Master Ryuho Okawa recites the sutra and describes its meaning paragraph by paragraph, sentence by sentence. From the creation of this great universe, the spirit world, and reincarnation, to the reason of human existence, and the difference between love and mercy, you will be able to learn the profound messages and the meaning of "The True Words Spoken By Buddha."

➲Available to members only. You may receive them at Happy Science local branches and shoja (temples) worldwide. See p.256.

ABOUT HAPPY SCIENCE

Happy Science is a global movement that empowers individuals to find purpose and spiritual happiness and to share that happiness with their families, societies, and the world. With more than 12 million members around the world, Happy Science aims to increase awareness of spiritual truths and expand our capacity for love, compassion, and joy so that together we can create the kind of world we all wish to live in.

Activities at Happy Science are based on the Principles of Happiness (Love, Wisdom, Self-Reflection, and Progress). These principles embrace worldwide philosophies and beliefs, transcending boundaries of culture and religions.

Love teaches us to give ourselves freely without expecting anything in return; it encompasses giving, nurturing, and forgiving.

Wisdom leads us to the insights of spiritual truths, and opens us to the true meaning of life and the will of God (the universe, the highest power, Buddha).

Self-Reflection brings a mindful, nonjudgmental lens to our thoughts and actions to help us find our truest selves—the essence of our souls—and deepen our connection to the highest power. It helps us attain a clean and peaceful mind and leads us to the right life path.

Progress emphasizes the positive, dynamic aspects of our spiritual growth—actions we can take to manifest and spread happiness around the world. It's a path that not only expands our soul growth, but also furthers the collective potential of the world we live in.

PROGRAMS AND EVENTS

The doors of Happy Science are open to all. We offer a variety of programs and events, including self-exploration and self-growth programs, spiritual seminars, meditation and contemplation sessions, study groups, and book events.

Our programs are designed to:
* Deepen your understanding of your purpose and meaning in life
* Improve your relationships and increase your capacity to love unconditionally
* Attain peace of mind, decrease anxiety and stress, and feel positive
* Gain deeper insights and a broader perspective on the world
* Learn how to overcome life's challenges

    ... and much more.

*For more information, visit **happy-science.org**.*

CONTACT INFORMATION

Happy Science is a worldwide organization with faith centers around the globe. For a comprehensive list of centers, visit the worldwide directory at *happy-science.org*. The following are some of the many Happy Science locations:

UNITED STATES AND CANADA

New York
79 Franklin St., New York, NY 10013
Phone: 212-343-7972
Fax: 212-343-7973
Email: ny@happy-science.org
Website: happyscience-usa.org

New Jersey
725 River Rd, #102B, Edgewater, NJ 07020
Phone: 201-313-0127
Fax: 201-313-0120
Email: nj@happy-science.org
Website: happyscience-usa.org

Florida
5208 8th St., St. Zephyrhills, FL 33542
Phone: 813-715-0000
Fax: 813-715-0010
Email: florida@happy-science.org
Website: happyscience-usa.org

Atlanta
1874 Piedmont Ave., NE Suite 360-C
Atlanta, GA 30324
Phone: 404-892-7770
Email: atlanta@happy-science.org
Website: happyscience-usa.org

San Francisco
525 Clinton St.
Redwood City, CA 94062
Phone & Fax: 650-363-2777
Email: sf@happy-science.org
Website: happyscience-usa.org

Los Angeles
1590 E. Del Mar Blvd., Pasadena, CA 91106
Phone: 626-395-7775
Fax: 626-395-7776
Email: la@happy-science.org
Website: happyscience-usa.org

Orange County
10231 Slater Ave., #204
Fountain Valley, CA 92708
Phone: 714-745-1140
Email: oc@happy-science.org
Website: happyscience-usa.org

San Diego
7841 Balboa Ave., Suite #202
San Diego, CA 92111
Phone: 626-395-7775
Fax: 626-395-7776
E-mail: sandiego@happy-science.org
Website: happyscience-usa.org

Hawaii
Phone: 808-591-9772
Fax: 808-591-9776
Email: hi@happy-science.org
Website: happyscience-usa.org

Kauai
3343 Kanakolu Street, Suite 5
Lihue, HI 96766, U.S.A.
Phone: 808-822-7007
Fax: 808-822-6007
Email: kauai-hi@happy-science.org
Website: happyscience-usa.org

Toronto
845 The Queensway
Etobicoke ON M8Z 1N6 Canada
Phone: 1-416-901-3747
Email: toronto@happy-science.org
Website: happy-science.ca

Vancouver
#201-2607 East 49th Avenue
Vancouver, BC, V5S 1J9, Canada
Phone: 1-604-437-7735
Fax: 1-604-437-7764
Email: vancouver@happy-science.org
Website: happy-science.ca

INTERNATIONAL

Tokyo
1-6-7 Togoshi, Shinagawa
Tokyo, 142-0041 Japan
Phone: 81-3-6384-5770
Fax: 81-3-6384-5776
Email: tokyo@happy-science.org
Website: happy-science.org

Seoul
74, Sadang-ro 27-gil,
Dongjak-gu, Seoul, Korea
Phone: 82-2-3478-8777
Fax: 82-2-3478-9777
Email: korea@happy-science.org
Website: happyscience-korea.org

London
3 Margaret St.
London,W1W 8RE United Kingdom
Phone: 44-20-7323-9255
Fax: 44-20-7323-9344
Email: eu@happy-science.org
Website: happyscience-uk.org

Taipei
No. 89, Lane 155, Dunhua N. Road
Songshan District, Taipei City 105, Taiwan
Phone: 886-2-2719-9377
Fax: 886-2-2719-5570
Email: taiwan@happy-science.org
Website: happyscience-tw.org

Sydney
516 Pacific Hwy, Lane Cove North,
NSW 2066, Australia
Phone: 61-2-9411-2877
Fax: 61-2-9411-2822
Email: sydney@happy-science.org

Malaysia
No 22A, Block 2, Jalil Link Jalan Jalil Jaya 2,
Bukit Jalil 57000, Kuala Lumpur, Malaysia
Phone: 60-3-8998-7877
Fax: 60-3-8998-7977
Email: malaysia@happy-science.org
Website: happyscience.org.my

Brazil Headquarters
Rua. Domingos de Morais 1154,
Vila Mariana, Sao Paulo SP
CEP 04009-002, Brazil
Phone: 55-11-5088-3800
Fax: 55-11-5088-3806
Email: sp@happy-science.org
Website: happyscience.com.br

Nepal
Kathmandu Metropolitan City Ward
No. 15,
Ring Road, Kimdol,
Sitapaila Kathmandu, Nepal
Phone: 97-714-272931
Email: nepal@happy-science.org

Jundiai
Rua Congo, 447, Jd. Bonfiglioli
Jundiai-CEP, 13207-340
Phone: 55-11-4587-5952
Email: jundiai@happy-science.org

Uganda
Plot 877 Rubaga Road, Kampala
P.O. Box 34130, Kampala, Uganda
Phone: 256-79-4682-121
Email: uganda@happy-science.org
Website: happyscience-uganda.org

ABOUT HAPPINESS REALIZATION PARTY

The Happiness Realization Party (HRP) was founded in May 2009 by Master Ryuho Okawa as part of the Happy Science Group to offer concrete and proactive solutions to the current issues such as military threats from North Korea and China and the long-term economic recession. HRP aims to implement drastic reforms of the Japanese government, thereby bringing peace and prosperity to Japan. To accomplish this, HRP proposes two key policies:

1) Strengthening the national security and the Japan-U.S. alliance, which plays a vital role in the stability of Asia.

2) Improving the Japanese economy by implementing drastic tax cuts, taking monetary easing measures and creating new major industries.

HRP advocates that Japan should offer a model of a religious nation that allows diverse values and beliefs to coexist, and that contributes to global peace.

*For more information, visit **en.hr-party.jp***

HAPPY SCIENCE ACADEMY
JUNIOR AND SENIOR HIGH SCHOOL

Happy Science Academy Junior and Senior High School is a boarding school founded with the goal of educating the future leaders of the world who can have a big vision, persevere, and take on new challenges.

Currently, there are two campuses in Japan; the Nasu Main Campus in Tochigi Prefecture, founded in 2010, and the Kansai Campus in Shiga Prefecture, founded in 2013.

Nasu Main Campus

Kansai Campus

ABOUT HAPPY SCIENCE MOVIES

BEAUTIFUL LURE

*Coming to Theaters
May 2021*

 With both beauty and wit, Maiko looks for a man who suits her. One night, she finds Taro, a candidate for the prime minister. Everything goes well as she plans, but Taro finds out that she is actually a "Youma," a foxy demon who destroys the country. What does fate hold for them?

For more information, visit **www.beautifullure.com**

TWICEBORN

 Satoru Ichijo receives a message from the spiritual world and realizes his mission is to lead humankind to happiness. He becomes a successful businessman while publishing spiritual messages secretly, but the devil's temptation shakes his mind and...

40 Awards from 8 Countries!

For more information, visit **www.twicebornmovie.com**

IMMORTAL HERO On VOD NOW

Based on the true story of a man whose near-death experience inspires him
to choose life... and change the lives of millions.

42 Awards from 9 Countries!

SPAIN
BARCELONA INTERNATIONAL
FILM FESTIVAL 2019
[THE CASTELL AWARDS]

SPAIN
MADRID INTERNATIONAL
FILM FESTIVAL 2019
[BEST DIRECTOR OF A FOREIGN
LANGUAGE FEATURE FILM]

ITALY
FLORENCE FILM AWARDS JUL 2019
[HONORABLE MENTION:
FEATURE FILM]

USA
INDIE VISIONS FILM FESTIVAL
JUL 2019 [WINNER (NARRATIVE
FEATURE FILM)]

ITALY
FLORENCE FILM AWARDS JUL 2019
[BEST ORIGINAL SCREENPLAY]

ITALY
DIAMOND FILM AWARDS JUL 2019
[WINNER (NARRATIVE
FEATURE FILM)]

...and more!

*For more information, visit **www.immortal-hero.com***

THE REAL EXORCIST On VOD NOW

56 Awards from 9 Countries!

STORY   Tokyo —the most mystical city in the world where
you find spiritual spots in the most unexpected places. Sayuri
works as a part-time waitress at a small coffee shop "Extra"
where regular customers enjoy the authentic coffee that the
owner brews. Meanwhile, Sayuri uses her supernatural powers
to help those who are troubled by spiritual phenomena one
after another. Through her special consultations, she touches
the hearts of the people and helps them by showing the truths
of the invisible world.

USA
GOLD REMI AWARD
53rd WorldFest Houston
International Film Festival 2020

MONACO
BEST FEATURE FILM
17th Angel Film Awards
2020
Monaco International Film Festival

NIGERIA
BEST FEATURE FILM
EKO International Film Festival
2020

THAI
BEST PRODUCTION DESIGN
Thai International Film Festival
2020

*For more information, visit **www.realexorcistmovie.com***

ABOUT IRH PRESS USA

IRH Press USA Inc. was founded in 2013 as an affiliated firm of IRH Press Co., Ltd. Based in New York, the press publishes books in various categories including spirituality, religion, and self-improvement and publishes books by Ryuho Okawa, the author of over 100 million books sold worldwide. For more information, visit _okawabooks.com_.

Follow us on:

Facebook: Okawa Books   **Twitter**: Okawa Books
Goodreads: Ryuho Okawa   **Instagram**: OkawaBooks
Pinterest: Okawa Books

---— **MEDIA** —---

OKAWA BOOK CLUB

A conversation about Ryuho Okawa's titles, topics ranging from self-help, current affairs, spirituality and religions.

Available at iTune, Spotify and Amazon Music.

Apple iTune:
https://podcasts.apple.com/us/podcast/okawa-book-club/id1527893043

Spotify:
https://open.spotify.com/show/09mpgX2iJ6stVm4eBRdo2b

Amazon Music:
https://music.amazon.com/podcasts/7b759f24-ff72-4523-bfee-24f48294998f/Okawa-Book-Club

BOOKS BY RYUHO OKAWA

RYUHO OKAWA'S LAWS SERIES

The Laws Series is an annual volume of books that are mainly comprised of Ryuho Okawa's lectures on various topics that highlight principles and guidelines for the activities of Happy Science every year. *The Laws of the Sun*, the first publication of the laws series, ranked in the annual best-selling list in Japan in 1987. Since then, all of the laws series' titles have ranked in the annual best-selling list for more than two decades, setting socio-cultural trends in Japan and around the world.

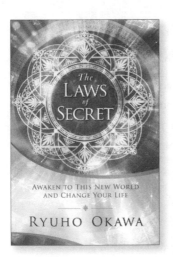

The 27th Laws Series

THE LAWS OF SECRET

AWAKEN TO THIS NEW WORLD AND CHANGE YOUR LIFE

Hardcover • 258 pages • $22.95
ISBN:978-1-943869-99-2

Our physical world coexists with the multi-dimensional spirit world and we are constantly interacting with some kind of spiritual energy, whether positive or negative, without consciously realizing it. This book reveals how our lives are affected by invisible influences, including the spiritual reasons behind influenza, the novel coronavirus infection, and other illnesses. The new view of the world in this book will inspire you to change your life in a better direction, and to become someone who can give hope and courage to others in this age of confusion.

---

*For a complete list of books, visit **okawabooks.com***

THE TRILOGY

The first three volumes of the Laws Series, *The Laws of the Sun*, *The Golden Laws*, and *The Nine Dimensions* make a trilogy that completes the basic framework of the teachings of God's Truths. *The Laws of the Sun* discusses the structure of God's Laws, *The Golden Laws* expounds on the doctrine of time, and *The Nine Dimensions* reveals the nature of space.

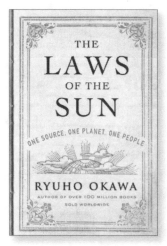

THE LAWS OF THE SUN

ONE SOURCE, ONE PLANET,
ONE PEOPLE

Paperback • 288 pages • $15.95
ISBN: 978-1-942125-43-3

IMAGINE IF YOU COULD ASK GOD why He created this world and what spiritual laws He used to shape us—and everything around us. If we could understand His designs and intentions, we could discover what our goals in life should be and whether our actions move us closer to those goals or farther away.

At a young age, a spiritual calling prompted Ryuho Okawa to outline what he innately understood to be universal truths for all humankind. In *The Laws of the Sun*, Okawa outlines these laws of the universe and provides a road map for living one's life with greater purpose and meaning.

In this powerful book, Ryuho Okawa reveals the transcendent nature of consciousness and the secrets of our multidimensional universe and our place in it. By understanding the different stages of love and following the Buddhist Eightfold Path, he believes we can speed up our eternal process of development. *The Laws of the Sun* shows the way to realize true happiness—a happiness that continues from this world through the other.

For a complete list of books, visit **okawabooks.com**

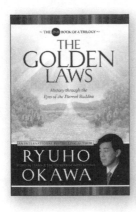

THE GOLDEN LAWS
HISTORY THROUGH THE EYES OF THE ETERNAL BUDDHA

Paperback • 201 pages • $14.95
ISBN: 978-1-941779-81-1

Throughout history, Great Guiding Spirits of Light have been present on Earth in both the East and the West at crucial points in human history to further our spiritual development. *The Golden Laws* reveals how Divine Plan has been unfolding on Earth, and outlines 5,000 years of the secret history of humankind. Once we understand the true course of history, through past, present and into the future, we cannot help but become aware of the significance of our spiritual mission in the present age.

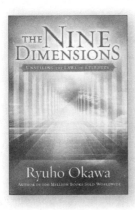

THE NINE DIMENSIONS
UNVEILING THE LAWS OF ETERNITY

Paperback • 168 pages • $15.95
ISBN: 978-0-982698-56-3

This book is a window into the mind of our loving God, who designed this world and the vast, wondrous world of our afterlife as a school with many levels through which our souls learn and grow. When the religions and cultures of the world discover the truth of their common spiritual origin, they will be inspired to accept their differences, come together under faith in God, and build an era of harmony and peaceful progress on Earth.

For a complete list of books, visit **okawabooks.com**

HIGHLIGHTED TITLE

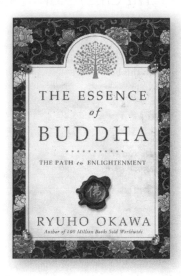

The Essence of Buddha

The Path to Enlightenment

Paperback • 208 pages • $14.95
ISBN: 978-1-942125-06-8

In this book, Ryuho Okawa imparts in simple and accessible
language his wisdom about the essence of Shakyamuni Buddha's
philosophy of life and enlightenment–teachings that have been
inspiring people all over the world for over 2,500 years. By offering
a new perspective on core Buddhist thoughts that have long been
cloaked in mystique, Okawa brings these teachings to life for
modern people. *The Essence of Buddha* distills a way of life that
anyone can practice to achieve a life of self-growth, compassionate
living, and true happiness.

---

*For a complete list of books, visit **okawabooks.com***

THE CHALLENGE OF THE MIND
AN ESSENTIAL GUIDE TO BUDDHA'S TEACHINGS: ZEN, KARMA AND ENLIGHTENMENT

Paperback • 208 pages • $16.95
ISBN: 978-1-942125-45-7

In this book, Ryuho Okawa explains essential Buddhist tenets and how to put them into practice. Enlightenment is not just an abstract idea but one that everyone can experience to some extent. Okawa offers a solid basis of reason and intellectual understanding to Buddhist concepts. By applying these basic principles to our lives, we can direct our minds to higher ideals and create a bright future for ourselves and others.

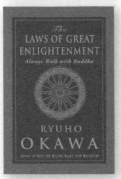

THE LAWS OF GREAT ENLIGHTENMENT
ALWAYS WALK WITH BUDDHA

Paperback • 232 pages • $17.95
ISBN: 978-1-942125-62-4

Constant self-blame for mistakes, setbacks, or failures and feelings of unforgivingness toward others are hard to overcome. Through the power of enlightenment we can learn to forgive ourselves and others, overcome life's problems, and courageously create a brighter future ourselves. This book addresses the core problems of life that people often struggle with and offers advice on how to overcome them based on spiritual truths.

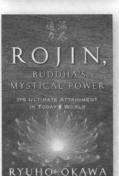

Scheduled to be published in Summer of 2021.

ROJIN, BUDDHA'S MYSTICAL POWER
ITS ULTIMATE ATTAINMENT IN TODAY'S WORLD

Paperback • 224 pages • $16.95
ISBN: 978-1-942125-82-2

In this book, Ryuho Okawa has redefined the traditional Buddhist term *Rojin* and explained that in modern society it means the following: the ability for individuals with great spiritual powers to live in the world as people with common sense while using their abilities to the optimal level. This book will unravel the mystery of the mind and lead you to the path to enlightenment.

*For a complete list of books, visit **okawabooks.com***

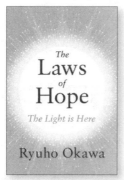

THE LAWS OF HOPE
THE LIGHT IS HERE

Paperback • 224 pages • $16.95
ISBN:978-1-942125-76-1

This book provides ways to bring light and hope to
ourselves through our own efforts, even in the midst of
sufferings and adversities. Inspired by a wish to bring
happiness, success, and hope to humanity, Okawa
shows us how to look at and think about our lives and
circumstances. He says that hopes come true when we
have the right mindset inside us.

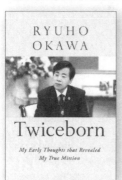

TWICEBORN
MY EARLY THOUGHTS THAT REVEALED
MY TRUE MISSION

Paperback • 206 pages • $19.95
ISBN: 978-1-942125-74-7

This semi-autobiography of Ryuho Okawa reveals the
origins of his thoughts and how he made up his mind
to establish Happy Science to spread the Truth to the
world. It also contains the very first grand lecture where
he declared himself as El Cantare. The timeless wisdom in
Twiceborn will surely inspire you and help you fulfill your
mission in this lifetime.

THE POWER OF BASICS
INTRODUCTION TO MODERN ZEN LIFE OF CALM,
SPIRITUALITY AND SUCCESS

Paperback • 232 pages • $16.95
ISBN:978-1-942125-75-4

The power of basics is a necessary asset to excel at any kind
of work. It is the power to meticulously pursue tasks with a
quiet Zen mindset. If you master this power of basics, you
can achieve new levels of productivity regardless of your
profession, and attain new heights of success and happiness.
This book also describes the essence of an intellectual life,
thereby reviving the true spirit of Zen in the modern age.

---

*For a complete list of books, visit **okawabooks.com***

THE UNHAPPINESS SYNDROME
28 HABITS OF UNHAPPY PEOPLE
(AND HOW TO CHANGE THEM)

Paperback • 189 pages • $15.95
ISBN: 978-1-942125-16-7

In this book, Ryuho Okawa diagnoses the 28 common habits of the Unhappiness Syndrome and offers prescriptions for changing them so that we can cure ourselves of this syndrome. With the prescriptions offered in this book, you can start to think and act in a way that attracts happiness and open a path to a positive, bright, and happy future!

THE LAWS OF SUCCESS
A SPIRITUAL GUIDE TO TURNING
YOUR HOPES INTO REALITY

Paperback • 207 pages • $15.95
ISBN: 978-1-942125-15-0

The Laws of Success offers 8 spiritual principles that, when put to practice in our day-to-day life, will help us attain lasting success. The timeless wisdom and practical steps that Ryuho Okawa offers will guide us through any difficulties and problems we may face in life, and serve as guiding principles for living a positive, constructive, and meaningful life.

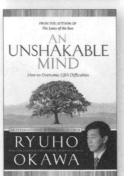

AN UNSHAKABLE MIND
HOW TO OVERCOME LIFE'S DIFFICULTIES

Paperback • 146 pages • $14.5
ISBN: 978-1-941779-67-5

This book describes ways to build inner confidence and achieve spiritual growth, adopting a spiritual perspective as the basis. With a willingness to learn from everything that life presents you, good or bad, any difficulty can be transformed into nourishment for the soul.

For a complete list of books, visit **_okawabooks.com_**

THE ROYAL ROAD OF LIFE
Beginning Your Path of Inner Peace, Virtue, and a Life of Purpose

THE LAWS OF HAPPINESS
Love, Wisdom, Self-Reflection and Progress

THE REAL EXORCIST
Attain Wisdom to Conquer Evil

THE HELL YOU NEVER KNEW
And How to Avoid Going There

WORRY-FREE LIVING
Let Go of Stress and Live in Peace and Happiness

THE STRONG MIND
The Art of Building the Inner Strength
to Overcome Life's Difficulties

HEALING FROM WITHIN
Life-Changing Keys to Calm, Spiritual, and Healthy Living

THE HEART OF WORK
10 Keys to Living Your Calling

INVITATION TO HAPPINESS
7 Inspirations from Your Inner Angel

For a complete list of books, visit **_okawabooks.com_**

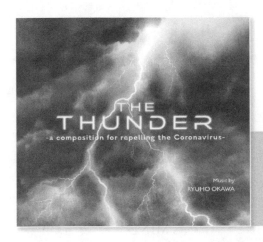

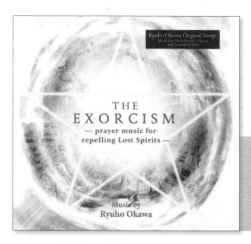